The Testimony of the Dead Man Walking

The Journal of Demario Jones:
47 Scars

By Demario Jones

This book is dedicated to God.

My people are destroyed for lack of knowledge: because thou hast rejected knowledge.

Hosea 4:6

The Testimony of the Dead Man Walking

The Journal of Demario Jones: 47 Scars

It All Starts Here...

Boom! Boom! Boom! Boom! Someone was banging on the front door in the middle of the night. *That's got to be the folks the way they beating on the door,* I said to myself as I quickly ran into the closet and tossed several bags of clothes on top of my body.

"Who the fuck that is beating on my goddamn door like that?" my girl Keya yelled. Keya stood about 5'4, milk chocolate skin, and curves to match. The closer she got to the door, the harder and louder the knocks got.

"This is the Jefferson County Sheriff Department, ma'am," answered a voice outside. "If you don't mind, we would like to ask you a few questions."

Keya peeked through the peephole and saw one chubby cop standing outside with several other police officers. "H-h-how can I help you?" she stuttered.

"Ma'am, are you the owner of this apartment?"

"Yes, sir, I am."

"So, you are Keya?"

"Yes, sir, I am."

"Well, ma'am," the chubby cop started as he pulled up his pants. "The reason we are here is concerning a homicide that took place yesterday on 16th Street West. And we were told that the suspect we are looking for by the name of Yo lives here. Is that true, ma'am?"

"No sir," said Keya in an innocent voice. "I don't know nobody by the name of Yo."

Oh shit, I thought to myself as I listened from upstairs. Even though the bags of clothes I was hiding under were heavy and I could barely breathe... I didn't give a fuck. I had to do whatever I could to keep the cops off of me. I was still on probation from the last time I got into it with the law.

"Ma'am, are you sure?" asked the chubby cop.

"Yes, sir, I'm positive."

"Well, we were told that he's your boyfriend, and he has been staying here, ma'am. So we are going to have to come in and search the apartment to make sure the suspect is not in there." He walked past her and took a look around the living room.

"What?" asked Keya nervously.

The cop narrowed his eyes. "Look, ma'am, are you sure before we start searching this apartment that there is no one inside?"

"Yes, sir. I don't know nobody by the name of Yo. My ol' man name is Mario Jones."

The cop took a long look at her and sighed. "Well, okay, ma'am. Just let me and my officers look around the apartment to make sure our suspect is not in there. And me and my officers will be out your way here shortly."

"Yes, sir," said Keya as the remaining officers came inside to search the apartment.

I was trying my best not to move a muscle or breathe too hard. My heart felt like it was trying to jump out of my chest as I heard the police getting closer to the closet I was hidden in. I could hear radios as they approached the closet door. Suddenly, it opened, and my heart dropped. I held my breath as the officer reached in and grabbed a couple of bags of clothes. *Damn, I'm gonna go to jail,* I thought to myself.

To my surprise, the police threw the bags of clothes back in the closet and shut the door. "The kid's room upstairs is clear," he shouted.

Damn, that was close, I said to myself as I laid in the closet waiting on the police to leave. Then I heard another police radio dispatch getting closer. *Shit! I thought they were leaving,* I thought to myself. The closet door swung open again, and the officer began pulling bags of clothes out of the closet. I felt the last one reveal my legs, and I knew I was busted.

"Freeze!" he screamed. "Don't move! Let me see your hands!"

I knew my dumb ass shouldn't have hidden in this closet, I thought to myself as I threw my hands up. *I should've jumped out the window, man damn.* The officer grabbed one of my hands and dragged me out of the closet. Forcefully, he shoved his knee into my back and twisted my arm.

"Don't fucking move," he growled as he put my hands behind my back and slapped on the handcuffs. All the other officers in the apartment ran upstairs into the room to see me pinned down on the floor.

"Yeah," said the chubby officer through gritted teeth. "That's our suspect because he has a gunshot wound to the hand."

Quickly, they picked me up off the floor and took me downstairs to sit me on the couch in the living room. Keya just stood there in silence.

"Ma'am, I thought you said you didn't know Yo?" said the chubby cop.

"His name ain't Yo," said Keya quietly.

"I thought you said no one else was in the apartment?"

"I just got home. I didn't know he was here."

"Just be quiet, ma'am," the cop that found me spat. "Because you're lying to the police."

They continued to search the apartment and found some other things stashed away. "And who does this belong to?" the chubby cop asked us as he pulled about 3 grams of heroin out of the purse that was tucked into the couch.

"I-I-I don't know," Keya stuttered, trying not to cry.

"Well, boy, what about you?" the chubby cop asked as he turned to me. I didn't say a word. I just sat there in silence.

"So, you don't hear me talking to you?" he asked. *Man, fuck you,* I thought to myself as I sat there not saying a word.

"Well, Keya, since it's in this purse with your identification, it's yours," he snapped as he aggressively put handcuffs on her also.

"What I'm going to jail for?" she cried.

"Possession of a controlled substance."

She sat there with her head hanging low. Just like that, I was on my way to the county jail along with my girl for capital murder.

Four Hours Later

Damn, I can't believe I'm back in this weak-ass county jail, I thought to myself. I was alone in my cell, watching the cars go up and down the freeway. It was cold inside the building, but I didn't care. I still couldn't believe I was back in here.

"Oh, now, seven cell," a deep raspy voice said across the way. The older man inside was trying to get my attention.

"Yeah, what's up?" I asked impatiently. "Hey, man, my name Sam," said the old man. "I sleep next door to you in eight cell."

I relaxed a little. "That's wassup. They call me Yo. Wassup, doe?"

"Nothing," sighed Sam. "I was just speaking to my neighbor. That's all, Yo."

"That's wassup."

"What floor you come off of, Yo?" asked Sam, breaking my thoughts.

"I came to the hole from booking."

15

"Oh yeah?"

"Yeah."

"Oh, so you just got locked up today," said Sam with interest.

"Yeah."

"Oh, okay. So why they sent you straight to the hole from booking? You must was cutting up in booking or something."

"No, I didn't do nothing. They just got mad at me because I wouldn't talk, and they can't figure out my real name. So, they got mad and sent me to the hole." Yeah, them folks real deal caught an attitude with me because I wouldn't talk."

"Straight up? That's crazy," said Sam. "So how many days you got in lock-up?"

"They said they going to leave me down here until they figure out who I am."

"That's crazy. Wow," sighed Sam as he shook his head.

"I'm already hip, though," I shrugged.

"So, what kind of case you got?" asked Sam.

"A cap."

"Damn, I hate to hear that."

"It's all good, ya hear me," I said quickly, not wanting him to feel sorry for me.

"So how old is you, Yo?"

"23."

"23. I got a grandson yo' age, youngster."

"Oh yeah?" Who would've thought.

"Now, youngster, you know they can give you the death penalty on that case, don't it?" asked Sam seriously.

"Yeah, I'm already hip, you hear me." I already knew what was up.

"Oh, okay. So, this ain't yo' first rodeo?" inquired Sam.

"Knawl, this my second time in the county."

"Okay, so you know what's going on then."

"Yeah, I'm hip."

"Oh, okay."

"Do you know around what time it is?" I had no idea how long it had been since I first got to this hell hole. It was dark outside, but that didn't say much.

"Yeah, it's 2:47 AM."

"That's wassup. So, what kind of case you got, Sam?" I asked, trying to shift the attention away from me and my problems.

"I'm back on a parole violation for having dirty urine," he answered casually.

"Oh okay. Shit, you should be finna get out any day now then, Sam."

"If it's the Lord's will, youngster, I will."

"If you don't got nothing but a little dirty urine, though… They don't hold niggas in jail for that."

"Yeah, but I got a life sentence on a murder case I caught in '84."

"84?" I asked surprised. "Damn, I wasn't even thought of yet. That was like 30 years ago. Shit, OG."

"Yeah. Exactly 28 years ago. I had a capital murder case, and I was in the same situation you in right now, youngster."

"Damn!" For the first time, I was completely speechless. Who would have ever thought that this cool-ass dude been threw all that.

"Yup," Sam continued. "Hell, I did 10 years on death row before I got this life sentence."

"Damn, straight up."

"Yep. 10 long years."

"So," I said curiously, "How you end up getting off death row?"

"By the grace of God, youngster. That's how."

I let out a breath. "It had to be." I already know it had to be something big for him to be able to go free after a cap charge. From what I heard, they not easy to beat. Especially not in Jefferson County jail; *that's* unheard of.

"It ain't no doubt about it, youngster. I just messed around and caught this dirty urine sample."

"Hmmm...so how it was when you was doing time on death row?"

I could hear Sam shift in his cell. "What do you mean, youngster?"

"Like, what did you do in a cell by yourself for 10 years?"

"Well..." said Sam slowly, "For the first seven years, I was mad at God and the whole world."

"Why you felt like that?"

"Well, youngster, I was waiting on my life to end. Day after day on death row...it takes a toll on your mental. I felt like God and everybody in the world had abandoned me, so I stopped reading my Bible and gave up on God."

"Oh, okay," I nodded. "Yeah, I can feel you on that on some." Hell, just the lil' stint I did awhile ago felt like an eternity. I could only imagine what a whole ten years must've felt like.

"Then, at the time youngster, the only person that was there for me—my mama—she was on her deathbed.

And I couldn't be there for her. When she died... that did it." Sam paused a second, trying to cover the pain in his voice.

"Damn, I hate to hear that," I said sympathetically. "So, what made you start back believing in God then?"

"Well, I remembered what my mama told me before she died. I didn't like what she said at the time, but like they say, youngster, the truth hurts."

"What she said?" I asked.

"She said, 'Sam, you can be mad at God the rest of your life and still die on death row and go straight to hell, or you can walk with God while you're alive on death row and go to heaven. Who knows, Sam, God might let you on the throne and out of prison if you go back on the walk with God.'"

"Damn, that's strong, ya hear me."

"I know," Sam smiled. "And here I am 28 years later. Sharing my testimony with you today in the county jail, youngster."

"Damn, that's some real shit, you hear me."

"I know, youngster. So, do you believe in Jesus?"

I paused for a moment. "Yeah, I believe in Jesus."

"Oh, okay. That's good. So, what was you doing out there? Was you going to church on the streets and stuff like that?"

"I'm not gonna even lie to you, Sam. The two years I was on the street, I probably went to church like two or three times, ya hear me."

"Well, at least you *went*. Some folks ain't never been."

That made me feel a little better. "You're right on something."

"So," Sam continued, "Do you read your Bible like that, youngster?"

I chuckled. "I am slipping on that too, Sam, ya hear me."

Sam laughed. "At least you honest, youngster."

"Ain't no need to lie, ya hear me."

"That's right," agreed Sam. "And that says a lot about you as a person, youngster."

"I'm already hip, but I don't like reading the Bible because I can't understand that stuff like *thou,* ya hear me."

"What do you mean you can't understand it?"

"I can't pronounce a lot of the words, and all that *thou* and *thee* makes it hard for me to comprehend words being said." Just thinking about it gives me a lil' anxiety. It be like I'm taking a page out of Shakespeare or something while I'm just trying to get a word.

"Oh, okay, I see what you're saying now, youngster. But you know they got a Bible that breaks all them big words down and replaces them with simple words. They took all the *thee* and *thou* out of it so you can understand it better."

I can't even lie. *That* sparked my interest. "Oh, yeah? They do? I never seen no Bible like that before, Sam, ya hear me."

"Yeah, it's called the New Living Translation version of the Bible. I got one over here in my cell, as a matter of fact, youngster. You can have it if you want it."

"Yeah, I'd like that."

"I'll send it over there by the runner when they pass out the breakfast trays."

"Alright. That's wassup. I need it, too. All this time I'm facing, ya hear me."

"That's right, youngster."

"Can't turn that down right there, Sam, ya hear me."

"It ain't no doubt, youngster. You know what to say."

"Shit, I'm already hip, ya hear me."

"That's right, youngster," smiled Sam.

"But check this out, Sam. I'm finna lay it on back because I'm tired."

"Okay, well, when the runner come for breakfast, I'm a get him to sit this Bible in your tray slot for ya."

"Alright, that's wassup."

"Okay, talk to you later, youngster."

"That's wassup, Sam," I responded as I sat down on the bed and looked at the wall. My eyes were heavy, but my mind was racing. *Damn,* I thought to myself. *I can't believe I'm in this bitch again. Fuck…. and my girl locked up too.* For the first time in years, I did something I hadn't done in a long time.

"God," I said softly, "Please. Please don't let my life end like this."

One Week Later

"Demario Jones!" yelled the officer as he pulled up to my cell door.

"Yeah, wassup?" I responded as I got up off the bed and went to the door. The officer had a tired look on his face as if he had been up late the previous night. He also had a strong cigarette smell coming from his clothes.

"How's it going, Mr. Jones? Are you ready to get out of lock-up?"

"Yeah," I said as I wiped the crust from my eyes.

"Okay, good. Well, you've been in lock-up about eight days now. If you plead guilty to this disciplinary for bad conduct, I'll give you 10 days in lock-up, which means you will get out of lock-up in two more days and be able to go upstairs to population."

I contemplated that for a second. What did I have to lose? "That's wassup," I said in agreeance.

"So, you pleading guilty? Yes or no."

"Yeah."

"Okay, good." The cop looked pleased with himself as he handed me a pen. "Well, just sign your name right here and put today's date right here, which is 6-22-12."

After I signed and dated my name, I gave the cop back the paperwork.

"All right, buddy. That's it," he said as he tucked the papers into his folder. "You'll be going upstairs on the 24th. Take it easy now."

As he walked away from my cell, I made my way back to my bed to relax. Looked like I was finally going to get out of lock-up.

"Yo, Sam," I called out.

"Yeah, what's up, youngster?" said Sam in a sleepy voice.

"Nothing. The police just pulled up to my cell and served me a disciplinary for bad conduct."

"Oh, yeah. How many days did they give you for that?"

"10 days."

"Oh, okay. You should be going upstairs soon then."

I let out a sigh of relief. "Yeah, in two more days."

"Well, that's good, youngster."

"I'm already hip, Sam, you hear me," I said confidently.

"Just don't forget what I told you when you go upstairs, now."

"What's that?" I asked, confused.

"About keeping God first and never stop having faith in Him no matter how bad things look. And He will see you through, youngster."

"Oh, yeah, Sam. You already know. I gotcha. Ya hear me."

"Okay. Just checking, youngster."

"I know," I said seriously, "but I appreciate you for opening my eyes, Sam. For real, ya hear me."

"Don't praise me, youngster," warned Sam. "Praise God. I'm just a vessel God used to deliver the message to you, so give God all the praise, youngster. You hear me and what I'm sayin'?"

"Yeah, you're right. I thank God for using you, ya hear me."

"That's right, and always remember, youngster. Just like God works through people for his work, the devil works through people for his work too."

"I'm already hip," I assured him.

"Just like we all was when we was blind to God's word. Our job as Christians is to spread the truth, so the blind can see."

"I'm already hip. That's why I got to start reading my Bible and get my life together."

"Look, youngster, grab your Bible and turn to second Timothy, 25-26."

"You said second Timothy, chapter 2, and what?" I asked as I grabbed my Bible off the table.

"Yeah, 2 Timothy, chapter 2 verses 25 and 26."

"Aite. Verse 25 and 26. I'm reading it now." I responded as I read it to myself in my cell.

"Sam, you don't play when it comes to this Bible. Everything you tell me, you can show me in the Bible. On something," I told Sam after I finish reading the verses.

"God don't play, youngster. That's Him working through me."

"You ain't lyin'. He don't, ya hear me."

"But, youngster, I'm about to take me a nap. I'll holler at you later on."

"Aite, that's wassup." With that, he was quiet, and I was back to my own thoughts in my cell. Something about that verse just kept replaying over and over again in my head.

"they will come to their senses and escape from the trap of the devil, who has taken them captive to do his will..."

Yeah, I know that I'm tired of the same ol' shit. I don't want this anymore. I think it's time to come to my senses...

First Day Out Of Lock-up!

"Jones. Demario Jones," the police said as he pulled up to my cell door. This cop was skinny with stringy blonde hair and brown eyes. He couldn't have been older than about 30 or 35.

"Yeah, what's up?" I said as I looked up and noticed him standing at the door.

"Pack your stuff up. You're going upstairs to the 9th floor to B-2."

"That's wassup. I'm already packed up," I said as I grabbed my stuff. He didn't know it, but I was happy to be getting out of there. Don't get me wrong, there ain't *no* part of being locked up that's fun. Still, if I had a choice, it wouldn't be in damn lock-up.

"All right, cool. I'll be back here shortly to take you upstairs to population, so be ready when I get back, buddy. I'll be back here to get you shortly." With that, he walked off from my cell.

I could barely contain my excitement. "Hey, Sam!" I called out.

"Yeah, wassup, youngster?"

"It's over with. I'm gone, man, ya hear me?"

"All right now, youngster. Remember what we talked about. Stay in that word, now, youngster."

"Alright. I gotcha, Sam."

"Alright, now. I'ma keep you in my prayers now, youngster, you hear me."

"That's what's up. I'm a keep you in mind too, Sam."

"Alright. Keep the faith now."

"That's wassup. I got you." Even though I barely knew this man a week, I felt kind of close to him because of what he had introduced to me. We don't really have a lot up here, so his giving me his Bible made me feel a certain way. Nothing bad, of course, but just…it's hard to explain. I was almost sad to have to leave Sam because I felt like it was so much more I could've learned from him. Regardless though, I know he fulfilled his primary purpose of reintroducing me to the gospel. Now, it was just up to me to do something with it.

Heading upstairs to the ninth floor!

Ping! Ding! was the sound of the elevator as me and the police went up each level until it came to a stop on the ninth floor. We both exited the elevator and walked up the hallway to the main sliding door, waiting on the police in the cube to let us in. The ninth floor consisted of nothing but violent offenders, and I was about to be joining them for a second time.

"Alright, buddy," said the cop. "Just walk up to that cube right there, and the officer will let you know what bed you were assigned to." The slider door rolled open, and I stepped through.

The cube looked a lot like the little cubicle you see on TV when people are in an office. Small, boring, and enough for one person. As I walked to the cube, the other officer looked at me out the corner of his eyes. He was a white guy with brown hair and freckles. His demeanor made it seem like he probably was a nerd in school. "What's your name?" he asked as I walked up to the cube.

"Demario Jones."

"Alright," he said as he typed my name into the computer. "You're assigned to B-block, cell block 2." He pushed the button to open up the block's main slider door.

"Alright. I just need me a blanket and some sheets."

"Hold on one second," said the cop as he went back into the cube. He came back a couple of minutes later with dingy white sheets and a thin blanket. "Here you go."

"I appreciate it," I said as I grabbed the blanket and two sheets before walking in B-block. It smelled musty. I slowly walked up the stairs into cell block 2, and he shut the door behind me. *Well, here I am,* I thought to myself. It was as basic as basic could get with a sink, toilet, and a bunk bed.

Out of the corner of my eye, I noticed somebody lying on the bottom bunk listening to the radio. He was probably south of 6 feet, lanky, and had hair that looked like it hadn't been cut in days. His beard was scruffy, and pieces of it weren't fully grown on the sides of his face.

"What's up bro, they called me Tez."

"That's what's up. They call me Yo," I responded as I grabbed my bed mat off the top bed and laid it on the floor along with my sheets, blanket, and Bible.

"You said Yo?"

"Yeah, Yo," I responded as I sat down on the bed mat on the floor.

"You must've come off of the 8th floor or something?"

"Yeah, I just got out of lock-up."

"Oh, yeah. How long did you spend in lock-up?"

"10 days."

"Oh, okay. So what did you do to go to lock-up?"

"Because when they brought me in from off the street," I said as I stretched out on my bed, "They couldn't figure out who I was. When they asked me, I wouldn't say nothing, so they got mad and put me in the hole 'til they figured out who I was."

Tez smirked in amusement. "So, how they figure out who you were then?"

"I guess when they fingerprinted me. I don't know, ya hear me."

"Damn, so where are you from?"

"I'm from Dolomite."

"Where that's at?"

"The west side."

"Okay," said Tez as he looked at the ceiling. "I'm from Eastlake.

"Oh, yeah. My nigga Lil' Billy from the Bay from there."

Tez shifted upright in his bed. This obviously piqued his interest. "You talking about brown skin Lil' Billy with the braids who had the blue cutlass?"

"Yeah, that's my nigga."

"Yeah, I know Lil' Billy. I fuck with Lil' Billy heavy. We were staying together and everything at one time."

"Oh yeah?"

"On God!" said Tez excitedly. "What he out there doing on the streets?"

"That nigga doing good since he got out the joint. He working and going to school."

"Oh. Billy was in prison?"

"Yeah, that nigga did five years in the joint."

"Oh, damn, I didn't know that. Damn…"

"Hell, yeah. He doing good out there now, though, ya hear me."

"That's wassup. I'm glad to hear that." Tez got quiet for a second as if he were contemplating about what to say next. "But look, if you don't mind me asking, what kind of case you got, fam?"

"A cap."

Tez's eyes narrowed. "Damn, for real?"

"Hell yeah."

"Damn. I hate to hear that, little bruh. That's what I'm back in the county for now. A cap."

"Oh yeah? Straight up?"

"Hell yeah. I've been down the road seven years on death row, but I'm finna get it up off me now. Thanks be to Allah."

"That's what's up, my nigga. On some." *Damn, seems like everybody I'm coming in contact with been on death row*, I thought to myself. It almost makes you wonder if this is some type of sign from God.

"I already know," said Tez, interrupting my thoughts. "But what's wrong with your hand? Why you got it wrapped up?"

"I got shot," I said flatly.

"Talking about like recently?"

"Yeah, I got shot on my case."

"On your case?"

"Yeah."

"Damn, fam. I hate to hear that. So you *just* got shot then?"

"Yeah."

"How many stitches you had to get for that shit?"

"I ain't got none."

Tez let out a low whistle. "Straight up? The police ain't take you to the hospital for that shit?"

"Yeah, but since I wouldn't talk at the hospital and give them my name, they got mad and brought me to the county like this." Now that he mentioned it, my hand was starting to get a little sore. Instinctively, I started to massage the area that had the wound.

"For real? So what the county jail nurse said when they seen it downstairs when you first came in?" prodded Tez.

"Nothing," I said in a flat tone. "She just wrapped it up for me and put me on the list to go to the free world hospital to get it treated." In case you ain't know, a free world hospital is something strictly for inmates— heavily guarded ad there's usually no visitors allowed.

"Damn, that's some fucked up ass shit, fam. They still supposed to let the folks stitch your hand up regardless. Shit, what if you couldn't talk and they ain't know it? You feel me, my nigga?"

"I'm already hip."

"I know that bitch hurt too, don't it?"

I looked at my hand. "Hell yeah."

"I know it, my nigga. That's why a nigga got to stay out this shit cause these folks don't give a fuck about a nigga."

"I'm already hip," I sighed, trying not to think about the pain in my hand. It seemed like every time he mentioned it, it would start to throb.

"Is this your first time in the county?" he asked,

"Hell no."

"Oh, okay. So you know what's what then. Shit, how old is you?"

"23."

"Oh, okay. You still young. You ever went to prison before?"

"Yeah, two years for burglary."

"So, you already know how this shit goes and shit. And they gave you two years?"

"Yeah. I did a 12 split 2."

Tez raised an eyebrow. "A 12 split 2? What kind of sentence is that?"

"Two years in prison and two on probation."

"Oh, okay. So did you ever get off probation?"

"Hell nah. I was supposed to get off in October."

"Damn. So, you can go back down the road then?"

"Shit, probably so," I sighed. Back to the same ol' shit.

"That might be a good thing, though. At least you ain't gotta sit in this weak ass county jail for no four or five years waiting to go to trial. At least down the road, you gonna eat good. You can get a cell phone, buy you some cigarettes off the store, and go outside and get you some air."

"Hell yeah, and I can get my GED and get me a little trade or something."

"I think by you being on probation and caught a cap, they gonna put you in lock-up at Kilby. And you can't get no GED or nothing back there."

"Damn, for real?" I said, a little disappointed. I was kind of hoping that something good would come out of all this.

"Hell yeah. If I'm not mistaken, I think that's how they do it, though. When you catch a cap on probation. That's why I thank Allah every day I'm finna get out this shit."

I heard about Allah, but I never really knew much about Islam or Muslims or anything like that. So since he wanna talk, I figured I might as well pick his brain a little bit. "You was a Muslim when you came to prison, or you became Muslim when you went to prison?"

"No, I was Christian before I went to prison. Why you ask?"

"I was just asking because I noticed you kept saying Allah."

"Oh, yeah, I'm Muslim. What you is a Christian?"

"Yeah, I believe in Jesus."

"Oh, okay. I believe in Jesus too. It's just I don't believe Jesus is God or the son of God. I believe he was a regular prophet like Moses and everyone else in the Bible."

"I'm already hip. Lil' Billy used to be trying to school me on that Muslim shit."

"Oh. Lil' Billy is Muslim?"

"Yeah, he had a little prayer rug on the streets and everything. Like, he's serious about that Muslim shit for real. He got mad at me one day on the streets about messing with his prayer rug."

"For real?" laughed Tez.

"Hell yeah," I chuckled. "I told that nigga you've been going to church all your life, now you get out the joint talking about you a Muslim and you don't eat pork. And he got that mad about that shit."

"Billy just know what's really going on now because he found out the truth, Yo," said Tez seriously. "I'm telling you now, fam. Just whenever you get a chance, read the Qu'ran. I'm telling you... I'm a living witness that all of it... that a lot is God, bro."

"I hear ya, but I believe in Jesus, ya hear me."

"I used to too because I was brought up Christian by my folks, so I believe in Jesus because that's how my folks raised me. But once I went to prison and study for myself and did my own research and seen all the flaws in the Bible and found out the Bible has been rewritten by the white man plenty of times and books missing out the Bible... I stopped going for that shit and studied and found what's best for me."

"That's wassup. I believe in Jesus, though, ya hear me," I repeated patiently.

"That's cool. But I'm just trying to help you, bro. That's how I'm gonna go home now off death row, bro, because of Allah, fam. On some."

"I hear ya," I said as I laid back on my bed. I thought about what Sam was telling me before I got out of lock-up. How the devil was going to attack me by using people to shake my faith in God. Who would've thought it would start happening so fast...

"Listen, bro," said Tez, interrupting my thoughts. "I got the best lawyer in the state of Alabama. Richard Jaffey. I know you know who that is."

"Nah, who is that?"

"What?" asked Tez surprised. "Let me show you who Richard Jaffey is." Tez reached under his bed and grabbed an old beaten up looking book. "This Richard Jaffey right here. Look how many cases he beat. Most of all, these cases are capital murder cases." He turned page after page, showing me pictures of the people Richard Jaffey helped get out of jail and all the cases he won in trial.

I couldn't help but be impressed. There were literally hundreds of former inmates in that book. "That's wassup," I said as I handed it back to him.

"Do you know how much Richard Jaffey charge for a cap case? The best lawyer in Alabama?"

"Hell no. How much he charge for that shit?"

"25 bands, fam," said Tez as he sat the book down on

the bed beside him. "And guess how much I had to pay him, my nigga? Nothing. He just picked my case up out of the blue for free."

"Damn! That's what's up. On something."

"That's why I'm telling you, fam. Allah is real, bruh, and you in this cell for me to help you. On Allah, bruh, for real."

"I hear ya, but look, I'm finna lay it on back and get me a little rest before we roll out the cell for dinner. I'll finish chopping it up with you on this later on, ya hear me."

"That's wassup."

"Aite, bet." As I finished making my bed up, I laid down feeling confused. After hearing Tez talk about Allah and how he got blessed by the lawyer out the blue and was finna get ready to go home... I started to doubt and question God. At the same time, I was hearing Sam in my head saying, *"Youngster, no matter what the devil try to throw at you, always keep your faith in God and watch what he do for you."* So, I asked God to show me he's the only true God if he truly is. Then, I grabbed my Bible and read it until I fell asleep.

Dinner Time!

Damn! Seem like a nigga just laid down, I said to myself as I got up off my bed and grabbed my toothbrush, toothpaste, and my face rag off the table. It feels like the same ol' routine. With sleep still in my eyes, I went straight to the sink to brush my teeth. *I can't believe I'm back in this bullshit right here again,* I thought as I looked in the mirror, disappointed with myself.

"What's up, lil' bro? You good?" asked Tez as he sat on the bottom bunk.

"Hell yeah, everything good," I responded with a mouth full of toothpaste.

"That's wassup. I was just asking because you look like you got something on your mind."

"I'm good, my nigga. I just look like this anyway, ya hear me." I finished rinsing the toothpaste out of my mouth.

"Aite, fam," chuckled Tez. "I'm just checking on you, my nigga."

"That's wassup. I appreciate it," I said as I wiped my eyes and the rest of the toothpaste with my face rag.

Once I was done, I sat down on my bed and put my shower flats on. I could hear it getting rowdy outside my cell, like they were watching a game or something.

"Everything is going to be straight, fam," said Tez as he got up off the bed and went to the sink.

"I'm already hip. This just how I am when I first wake up in the county jail facing the death penalty, ya hear me."

Tez busted out laughing. "Nigga, yo ass crazy!"

"Bruh, I'm forreal. Shit."

"I know how you feel, my nigga. You gonna be straight."

"That's wassup. I'm gonna go out here in the day space," I said as I stood up.

"Alright, that's wassup."

With that, I walked out of the cell and stood up against the wall.

"Bring out your Bible if you coming to prayer call!" somebody said out loud in the day space. I was interested, so I went back in my cell, got my Bible off the table, and went back into the day space and stood back up against the wall. As soon as I posted up, I started hearing voices in my head telling me to take my Bible back in my cell and not to go to prayer call. At the same time, I was hearing Sam saying, *"Youngster, no matter what, keep your faith in God and stay around people who can continue to teach you God's word and don't let that devil trick you with his deceptive lies."* The more I get tested, the more I kept hearing Sam's words echo in my head.

"All right, y'all got five more minutes on them doors. The longer y'all stay in them cells, the longer I'ma keep them TVs off," the police said over the loudspeaker.

"Man, y'all niggas hurry up and come out them cell's man, so the police will go and turn the TV on!" somebody yelled out loud in the day space.

"Man, fuck them police! They can have that motherfucking TV!"

"Yeah, niggas kill me trying to do the police job! I know y'all on nigga's paperwork right now. Ol' working for the state ass nigga," somebody responded back.

"Man, I'm just trying to get the TV on so I can catch the news cause I got people out there in the world, my nigga."

"Shit, nigga, if you care so much, then you should've stayed out there in the world with your folks!"

"Yeah, niggas kill me. When y'all come to jail, *now* all of a sudden y'all care so much about your folks. When y'all was out there stealing your children's toys from under the Christmas tree to go buy that dope ol' crack-head ass nigga!"

Everybody in the day space busted out laughing. It was like one big family. You had the big ones, the small ones, the ones with muscle, and the ones who looked like they don't eat much. Dark, light, black, and white—it didn't make a difference up in here. You can get cussed out, bullied, or even left completely alone. It was all up to you and how you carried yourself. What I learned was not to look like no punk but to not act like you wanna fight everybody either. It's about balance.

"You got everything you need out the cell before I lock the door, lil' bruh?" asked Tez as he poked his head out of the cell door.

"Yeah, I'm good to go. You can shut it." I stood up against the wall staring at the black wall phone close to the doors. I debated on calling my mama. Knowing how she is and with pressure already on my back... I didn't need that. So, I just took a seat on the floor beside my cell and set my Bible down beside me.

Lord, please help me out of here. I can't live the rest of my life like this, man, forreal, I said silently to God.

"Alright. Everybody on your feet and stand in front of your cell. It's count time," said the police as they walked through the block. Quickly, I got up off the floor and stood by my cell. One thing you didn't want to do is test the police about count time. I've seen people get they ass beat for not being where they were supposed to be during count.

While they came around looking at each inmate in the cellblock, I stood there saying to myself, *Where a nigga going nine floors up and a million locked doors?* Yeah, these folks are crazy.

"Alright, y'all good. Count clear!" the police said after they finished counting and walked out the cellblock. A few inmates turned their noses up at them as they walked away.

"Prayer call! Prayer call!" somebody yelled out loud in the day space of the cellblock. Finally! I grabbed my Bible off the floor and headed downstairs for prayer call. It was a big room with nothing really in it but a couple of chairs. Matching the rest of the "aesthetic," it was boring, gray, and dull.

"Hey, how are you doing? I'm glad you came, my brother. I'm Jamaca," said a short dark skinned man with a fade as I walked up to the prayer circle.

"I'm doing alright. I'm Yo," I responded as I started shaking his hand.

"Okay. Good. God bless you, Yo. Thanks for coming to prayer call. God's got a message for you."

"That's wassup," I said, feeling good about the atmosphere in the room. There were about 9 other inmates in the room with me. Nothing really stood out about any of them—they all looked like normal guys. One did have a scar across his left eye but that's about it.

"Alright. Let's all join hands and bow our heads for prayer," said Jamaca. We all bowed our heads, and everybody began saying the Lord's prayer except me because I didn't know it. I just stood there with my head down and waiting on everybody to finish praying.

"Alright," said Jamaca. "At this time, if you want to sit down, you can, or if you want to stand up, that's fine too. But go ahead and grab your Bible for me."

I went ahead and took a seat with my Bible on the floor next to Scarface as Jamaca started speaking. "Now today, I'm going to talk about standing firm and never giving up and keeping your faith in God no matter what." His expression went from friendly to dead serious. This was about to get deep. I thought about what Sam was telling me before I got out of lock-up. "Now, today, I'm going to talk about standing firm on God's word. Amen?" continued Jamaca.

"Amen," we said in unison.

"Now, as y'all listen to me, I want y'all to realize that God is bringing His word to y'all through me by the Holy Spirit that lives in me. He's trying to reach each and everyone in this prayer circle today. Now, y'all could have went and played dominoes or cards or went and watched TV or got on the phone or did *anything* other than coming to prayer call, but y'all came to hear the word of God. And He has a message for each and every one of y'all today.

"Now, some of y'all may have a strong relationship with God and got the wisdom, knowledge, and understanding to know that when you hear the word preached, it helps your faith grow. And it helps you stand firm when the devil tries to steal God's word from you and make you not believe in God's word. But some of y'all may not have the wisdom, knowledge, or understanding of these things at all. So, when the devil attacks you with his tricky lies, you start to doubt God's word because you don't have the knowledge of what the devil is doing.

"You see, the devil been tricking people for years and years before we was born, and he knows our weaknesses. So, we gotta be aware when he attacks us and fight back with God's word. But in order for you to fight back with the word of God, you gotta study God's word on your own free time to build a strong personal relationship with the Creator, so you'll know how to fight the enemy by knowing God's word.

"Now turn to John chapter one in your Bibles, and when you find it, let me hear you say amen."

Everybody in the prayer circle grabbed their Bibles and turn to John chapter one and said Amen like Jamaca asked us to do. I think we all were intrigued with how God was going to use this man to get through to us tonight. No one was laughing, joking, or even smiling. The only look we had on our faces was one of anticipation. We were eager to hear what was next.

"Alright, I'm going to read verse one through 5," Jamaica said as he began reading:

[1]In the beginning the Word already existed. The Word was with God, and the Word was God.[2] He existed in the beginning with God.[3] God created everything through him, and nothing was created except through him.[4] The Word gave life to everything that was created,[a] and his life brought light to everyone. [5] The light shines in the darkness, and the darkness can never extinguish it.

(John 1: 1-5, NLT)

"Now, the reason I wanted to show you all this is because I want y'all to realize this very book, yes *this* Bible, is the word of God which is God Himself right here in our hands. Not half of it or most of it, but all of this Bible is God. That's why I was telling you all earlier that in order to learn God and build a strong relationship with God, you gotta study His word daily and learn Him by reading His word, which is Him. Amen. And with that being said, does anyone have any questions?"

As he looked around at everybody in the prayer circle, I slowly raised my hand. "Yeah, I do."

"Go ahead, Yo," encouraged Jamaca. "What's your question?"

"Today, I was talking with my celly. He is Muslim, and he was basically telling me I believe in the wrong God and that Jesus is the white man's god, and that's how they control their black man. He also said that the Bible has been rewritten several times, and books are missing out of it. He said that I need to study for myself to find out the truth, and I'm not gonna lie... it made me start to doubt God and second guess because, to be honest, the only reason I believe in God is because that's how my people raised me—"

"Enough said, Yo," interrupted Jamaca. "I'm glad you came to prayer call and even more glad you were bold enough to raise your hand and share with us what's going on. But I want you to realize that the devil is our enemy, and he is going to do anything--and I mean *anything*--to steal your belief in God. Because he knows once he's got your belief, he's got your soul. But, Yo, I'm here to tell you from experience that Jesus is the only true God. I don't know what kind of case you got or what you are in the county jail for, but just continue to keep your faith in God and live according to His word and watch what God does for you, my brother. I promise you, you won't regret it. Do you hear me, my brother?"

"Yeah." That was all I needed. I just needed a little bit of clarification that I was on the right path.

"Alright, good. And always remember, Yo, your God is able to do anything. All you gotta do is trust and believe in Him, and He will. And I put my life on it."

"Okay, that's what's up," I responded as chills came over me.

"Well, I'm glad you came to prayer call, my brother, and I ask you to continue to come every day to hear God's word. So you can continue to grow stronger in the faith. Okay?"

"I am."

"Okay, good, but I know you all are ready to get on the phone or whatever else you have to do today before we roll back in our cells in a few minutes. I'm gonna go ahead and let you all go for today. Do anybody have any more questions before we pray out?" asked Jamaca as he looked out in the prayer circle. Nobody said a word.

"Alright. Well, everybody on your feet. Let's join hands so we can pray out." With that, everybody stood to their feet and joined hands. Jamaca began saying the

Lord's prayer along with everyone else. Afterward, everyone shook hands and went their separate ways.

"Thanks for coming to prayer call. I hope to see you again tomorrow," said Jamaca as he shook my hand.

"That's what's up. I'ma come. I appreciate you for helping me on that too, ya hear me," I said with sincerity.

"No problem. Anytime. Thank you for asking, my brother. That was appreciated."

"That's what's up. I appreciate it."

"Alright. God bless. See you tomorrow."

"God bless you too," I said as I walked away from Jamaca and went upstairs to sit on the floor in front of my cell. My mind was racing. I was feeling proud of myself because I went to prayer call and didn't let those voices in my head stop me from going. If I didn't, I wouldn't have ever learned what I learned about the devil and how he played games.

"Demario Jones report to the slider. You got an attorney visit. Demario Jones report to the slider door for your attorney visit," the police said over the loudspeaker in the day space. I got up and headed down the stairs and out the slider door. I was met by two men who looked like presidents. Both of them had on three-piece suits, ties, and shiny leather shoes. One of them was white with a shiny bald head. He had a clean-shaven face and his brown eyes looked like he didn't get a lot of sleep. The second guy had curly brown hair that was gelled down to his head, green eyes, and a thick mustache that tickled the top of his upper lip as he talked.

"Hey, how are you doing, Mr. Jones? My name is Bob Johnson. I'm your attorney on your case," said the bald one as he reached out and shook my hand.

"That's what's up. I'm doing alright," I responded.

"And this is your other attorney who will be working with me on your case. Mr. Jim O'Kelly." I shook his hand vigorously and he gave a crooked smile.

"How's it going?" asked Mr. O' Kelly as he shook my hand.

"I'm doing alright," I said flatly. Well, at least they *looked* the part.

"Let's walk over here and have a seat," said Mr. Johnson as we walked into the visitation area. There were maybe 4 other sets of inmates in there. One was visiting what looked like his wife or something, two of them visiting probably lawyers, and the last was with an older gentleman who more than likely was his father.

"Okay, well, we're your lawyers on your case, Mr. Jones," said Mr. Johnson, "and the reason you have two lawyers is because on a capital offense, you have to have two."

"That's what's up," I said calmly.

"Now, a capital offense consists of a murder and another crime in the act of the murder."

"I'm hip."

"And you were charged with a murder and a robbery which makes it a capital offense," continued Mr. Johnson.

"Okay, I know."

"We're not saying you did anything, but if you are found guilty of a capital offense, you can only get sentenced to life without parole or the death penalty. Do you understand?"

"I'm hip." These folks weren't telling me anything that I didn't already know.

The two lawyers narrowed their eyes. "You seem pretty calm. You must know about this already?" asked Mr. Johnson.

"Yeah, I'm already hip to what's going on."

"Okay, good. Now that we got that out the way, we need to know did you make a statement to the police?"

"No, I didn't."

"Well, good. And are you sure you didn't give any statement whatsoever?"

"I'm positive. I didn't."

"Well, that's a big plus, Mr. Jones," smiled Mr. O'Kelly. "What happened to your hand?"

I winced as I thought about the pain in my hand. "I got shot.

"On this case?" asked Mr. O'Kelly.

"Yeah."

Mr. Johnson's eyes widened. "That's a self-defense wound all day!" he said excitedly.

"I'm already hip."

"Well, we got two weeks before we go to court to find

out what's what," said Mr. Johnson. "One more thing. Before me and Mr. O' Kelly head out, we have to ask were you on parole or probation or anything like that before you caught this case."

"Yeah, I was on probation."

"Okay, and what judge did you have while you were on probation?"

"I had Lauren Pedro."

Mr. Johnson's eyes widened. "You said Lauren Pedro?"

"Yeah, Lauren Pedro."

"Okay. Well, that's it for today, Mr. Jones. Do you have any questions or anything for me or Mr. O'Kelly before we leave?"

"I'm good."

"Well, okay then, buddy. See you in two weeks for court." With that, both lawyers searched across the table to shake my hand. I got up and walked out of the visitation room with them. That look on my lawyer's face when I told him what judge I had made me feel a bit uneasy. Was there something that I needed to know about her? Was she a stickler for certain things? A million and one questions ran through my head. I didn't

know what was about to happen, but all I knew was
that I had to keep my faith.

Court Day

Ding! was the sound of the elevator coming to a stop on the courtroom floor.

"Everybody off!" yelled the officer. He held the elevator doors open for several other inmates and me to exit into the hallway. All you could hear was the sound of handcuffs and shackles jingling back and forth while we shuffled our feet across the floor of the courthouse.

"Alright, there will be no talking in the courtroom unless you are talking to the judge. Does everybody understand?" the officer said to us as we stood in the hallway.

We nodded our heads at the same time in agreeance.

"Okay, when we walk in this courtroom, it's some seats to the left. That's where you all are to be at all times. Did everybody get that?" the officer asked.

"Yeah," we answered in unison.

"Does anybody gotta use the restroom? If so, go ahead and use it now while we are right here by the restroom because once you go in this courtroom, ain't no coming to the restroom." He quickly unlocked the restroom door and let some of the inmates go in and use the bathroom. "What about you? You ain't gotta use the restroom?" he asked as he looked at me.

"No, I'm straight," I said quickly as I stood there and waited on the other inmates to finish.

Once everyone came out, the cop did a quick head-count. "Alright. Remember when y'all go in this court-room to sit in the seats on the left." With that, he un-locked the courtroom door and motioned for us to walk inside.

We all walked in and sat in our seats. As soon as I sat down and looked around, I noticed my momma smil-ing and waving at me. I also noticed my co-defendants baby mama and his little girl and brother were waving at him. When they looked at me, they had a stale look on their faces that caught my attention. I couldn't let that break my concentration. I just looked off and paid it no mind.

"Hey there, Mr. Jones," greeted Mr. Johnson as he walked up to me and shook my hand. Today he was sporting a grey suit with a teal blue tie. He also had a brown Rolex on his wrist. "You are looking good and healthy today."

"Appreciate it. You don't look too bad yourself for an old man," I said while laughing and returning his handshake.

"Well, thank you, buddy. I'm doing pretty good for an old man. Are any of your family members here in the courtroom with you today?"

"Yeah, my momma is."

"Okay, good. Let me go in the back for a quick second and holler at the judge and see if she will let us go in the visitor room so we can have a talk."

"Okay, that's what's up."

"Alright, buddy, I'll be back shortly. Sit tight." Mr. Johnson walked off and headed to the back to have a talk with the judge. While he was gone, all I could do was think about everything that led to this point. It still felt like I was in a bad dream and couldn't wake up. I feel like I was doing so good this time around, trying to keep myself out of trouble and whatnot. Still, I'm right here back in this jail, and this time…I could lose my freedom for good. *God, please just help me through this,* I prayed silently.

Mr. Johnson came back with a smug look on his face. "Okay, now here's what we got here," he started. "The judge said we can go to the back for a little while after she gets through with us."

I couldn't help but smile a little bit. At least *something* good seemed to be in the works.

"Okay," I responded.

"Now, show me which lady is your mom. I need to know so I can let her know to wait up after the judge is done so we can have a talk in the back."

"That's my mama right there with the red shirt on." I pointed. "Right there."

"Okay. Let me go talk with her, and I'll be right back to let you know what she said."

He walked off to let my mama know what was up. The judge came from out the back and took her seat. She was a petite white woman with jet black hair and wore black-rimmed glasses in front of her brown eyes. "Hello, how's everyone doing today," she asked as she started looking through papers on her desk. "I'm Judge Vincent.

Mr. Johnson came back over to where I was sitting. "I just talked with your mom and let her know to sit around once the judges get through with us," he said quickly.

"That's what's up," I said.

"Okay, let's see here. Do I have a Demario Jones in court today?" asked the judge.

"Yes, ma'am. He's here, judge."

"Okay, are you and Mr. O'Kelly ready to get started?"

"Yes, ma'am, judge. I need one second to go get Mr. O'Kelly from out the back."

"Okay," said Judge Vincent.

"Thanks, judge," said Mr. Johnson as he went in the back of the courtroom to get Mr. O'Kelly.

"You're welcome, Bob," she said cheerfully as she took a sip out of her cup on her desk and set it back down.

A few minutes later, Mr. Johnson came back with Mr. O'Kelly practically on his heels. "Sorry about that, judge. How are you doing today?"

"I'm doing wonderful, Mr. O'Kelly. Thanks for asking," Judge Vincent responded with a smile on her face.

"Hey, Demario," whispered Mr. Johnson. "Come on. You got to come up front with me and Mr. O'Kelly," murmured Mr. Johnson as he held me up out of my seat and walked me to the table in front of the courtroom.

He pulled a chair out and help me sit down.

"Okay, what about you, Mr. Robert? Are you ready to get started?" she asked the District Attorney.

"Yes, judge. I am," the D.A. responded with a blank look on his face.

"Okay, wonderful. You may begin, Mr. Robert," said the judge smiling.

"Okay," started the D.A., "There was a murder and robbery that took place on 6/15/12 in the Center Point area in Jefferson County that Mr. Jones here played a major part in, judge."

"Okay, do you have any statements, Robert?" asked Judge Vincent.

"Actually, yes, judge. I have two statements. One from Mr. Jeremy Bell, which is Demario Jones's co-defendant, and one from Julia Bell, which is Jeremy Bell's mom."

"Okay, but do you have a statement from Demario Jones?"

"No, judge. I do not. He refused to make a statement. As a matter of fact, when he was captured a day later, he refused to even tell the officers his name."

"Well, okay. Thanks, Robert," said Judge Vincent. I

looked over and noticed my co-defendant crying real tears. "Well, how do you all plead?"

"Not guilty, judge," smiled Mr. Johnson.

She nodded her head. "Oh well, that's it. Until next time, Bob and Mr. O'Kelly."

"Okay. Thanks, judge. And can me and Mr. O'Kelly still go to the back and have a talk with Demario and his mother?"

"Well, yes. Go right ahead, Bob."

"Thanks, judge."

"One more thing before you and Mr. O'Kelly go to the back. Was Mr. Jones on parole probation or anything like that?" she asked.

Mr. Johnson paused. "Thanks for asking, judge. As a matter of fact, he was on probation. Sorry about that," apologized Mr. Johnson.

The judge narrowed her eyes. "And what judge did he have while on probation?"

Mr. Johnson looked up at the ceiling for a second before answering. "I think it was Lauren Pedro's courtroom," he said slowly.

"Okay," she said as she smacked her lips. "I want to let her know, and it will be up to her if she wants to revoke his probation or not. But other than that, you and Mr. O'Kelly are good to go to the back and have a talk with Mr. Jones's mother."

"Alright, thanks so much, judge," said Mr. Johnson as he held me up out of my seat and told my mom to come to the back in the visitor room. The judge gave a slight nod and went back to her notes.

As soon as we got in, he introduced himself. "Hey, how you doing. I'm Bob Johnson—"

"And I'm Mr. O'Kelly," cut in Mr. O'Kelly.

"Nice to meet you all. I'm Yolanda Terry," my mom stated as she shook both of my lawyers' hands.

"Well," started Mr. Johnson, "What we did today was plead not guilty and waived his case upstairs to the grand jury to see if they have enough evidence to indict him, which we know they probably will due to the fact that Demario's co-defendant Jeremy Bell and his mother Julia Bell made a statement. And—"

"Okay, so let me ask you all this," cut in my mom. "How long is my son going to be in jail?"

Mr. Johnson ran his hand over his bald head. "Once

you waive the case upstairs to the grand jury, it usually takes up to six months," he said slowly.

"Oh, okay. So how long will it take for all this to be over with, period?" asked Mama.

"Well...to be honest with you... that's hard to say right now," Mr. O'Kelly admitted. "They can come back, and with the grand jury...it can be either six months, or it could take up to four or five years to be going to trial."

Mama let out a whistle. "Oh, my Lord," she said, trying to fight back her tears. "How much time is the judge trying to give him?"

"Well, she hasn't offered any time yet, but on capital offenses, you can only get two things. That's life without parole or the death penalty," explained Mr. O'Kelley.

"Lord, have mercy!" cried Mama. "That's why I used to stay on you like I did 'cause I didn't want you to go through this." She couldn't hold back the tears as they began to fall from her cheeks.

"Sorry to tell you that, Miss Terry," said Mr. Johnson sincerely. I know he meant well, but she needed to just hear everything out of my mouth.

"Mama, don't start all that. I ain't got time for that," I said, trying to console her. "You can go on. I'll call you later on tonight." I just wanted her to leave at that point.

"Alright. Just know that Mama loves you, and I'll put some money on your books when I get paid Friday," she added as she got ready to go.

I looked up at her and tried to put on a fake smile. "Alright, Mama. I love you too."

"Alright. Make sure you call me tonight, and nice meeting y'all. Mr. Johnson and Mr. O'Kelly."

"Nice meeting you too," the lawyers responded in unison as they shook her hand.

"Alright, you have a blessed day." With that, she walked out of the visitor's room and was gone. I couldn't help but feel indifferent about everything. You would think that the possibility of death row would have me feeling really uneasy or even scared, but I was just…indifferent. It just didn't seem like it was real.

"Well, Mr. Jones," said Mr. Johnson. "The next thing we should be going to is a probation revocation hearing shortly. Probably a week or two from now in Judge Pedro's courtroom to see what she's going to do about your probation."

"Alright, that's wassup."

"How much time did you have left on probation?" inquired Mr. Johnson.

"Three months."

Mr. Johnson's eyes lit up. "Oh, that's not bad. She probably will let you kill the rest of that time in the court in the county jail. Then again, she might revoke you and send you back to prison."

"That's wassup," I responded flatly.

"Well, do you have any questions for me or Mr. O'Kelly?"

"No, I'm good.

"Well, okay, Demario. Come on, let's be on our way because me and Jim got some other cases in another courtroom we have to go to."

As I got up from the table, Mr. Johnson added one more thing. "Oh yeah. Me and Mr. O'Kelly will come and see you sometime before the week is out to let you know when we gotta go to court in Judge Pedro's courtroom about your probation."

"Alright, that's wassup," I said as I shook both of their hands.

"Take it easy up there in that jail, buddy," said Mr. O'Kelly before they both disappeared out the court-room.

I sat down in my seat with the rest of the inmates and waited on the police to take me back upstairs to the 9th floor. I looked over at Jeremy and noticed that he was still crying. *The fuck this nigga crying for?* I thought to myself.

"Alright, everybody, let's go," the officer said as he approached us. We all got up out of our seats and headed back to the elevator with the officer.

Jeremy finally locked eyes with me for the first time as we were walking to the elevator. "I'm s-s-sorry, b-b-bro," he stammered, "I'm j-j-just trying to go h-h-h-home to my little g-g-g-girl, bro."

[8]Finally, all of you should be of one mind. Sympathize with each other. Love each other as brothers and sisters.[a] Be tenderhearted, and keep a humble attitude. [9]Don't repay evil for evil. Don't retaliate with insults when people insult you. Instead, pay them back with a blessing. That is what God has called you to do, and he will grant you his blessing. [10] For

the Scriptures say, "If you want to enjoy life and see many happy days, keep your tongue from speaking evil and your lips from telling lies. [11] Turn away from evil and do good. Search for peace, and work to maintain it. [12]The eyes of the Lord watch over those who do right, and his ears are open to their prayers. But the Lord turns his face against those who do evil.

(1 Peter: 3:8-12, NLT)

"You good, my nigga. I'm blessed, bruh, just pray and keep ya head up, bruh, ya hear me," I responded, being obedient to God's word.

"Dats wassup, bruh. Pray for me, my nigga. Forreal," begged Jeremy.

"Aite, I gotcha, bruh. Be bless."

"Aite. Thank ya, bruh. I'ma pray for you too." As he said that, the elevator came to a stop.

"Alright," spat the officer, "Everybody off who sleep on 8." About 11 or 12 guys stepped off before the elevator doors rolled back shut. Once we got to the 9th floor, the officer let me off the elevator and watched me walk through the main slider door to the cube with the other officer.

"Alright, I got 'em," said the cube officer as the main slider doors rolled back shut. The cube officer was black, muscular, and might have been about 6'3. This man looked like he took his job way too seriously. He quickly took my handcuffs and shackles off and rolled open the slider doors to my cell block to let me go back in. My cellmate was in there reading a magazine.

"Wassup, lil' bruh? What they was talking 'bout when you went to court today?" asked Tez.

"Nun. They just waive my case upstairs to the grand jury," I responded as I walked to my bed.

"Oh ok. So was yo' co-defendant in there witcha?"

"Yeah, that nigga was in there with me."

"Oh yeah, so did he keep it solid?"

"Long story short... I need a Newport." I responded.

Tez chuckled. "Damn, my nigga. I hate dem ole bitch

ass niggas, bruh. Forreal fam."

"I'm blessed, my nigga, I ain't even trippin', ya hear me."

"I hear ya, lil' bruh, but you gotta get you some paid lawyers, lil' fam. Forreal, dog," he said seriously.

"It's all good, ya hear me."

"Look. I'm not trying to bring you down, fam. I just know how these folks play with a nigga life. They play a dirty game, fam."

"I'm blessed, my nigga. Ya hear me."

"Did yo' momma show up for court today?"

"Yeah, she came."

"Dat's good 'cuz you gotta show them folks you got folks on the outside that love ya, my nigga."

"I'm already hip. I seen my gul ass too on the way to court today."

"Oh, you did?" asked Tez. He was interested to hear this shit. When you locked up any type of news like that is something to talk about.

"Hell yeah. I stuck my tongue down her throat and er-rthang," I responded proudly.

Tez was intrigued. "Nigga gone on with that bullshit," he laughed. "How you pull that off?"

"You know when we get off the elevator downstairs, and they make us get up against the wall?"

"Yeah. In front the holding tank where they back us in until we get ready to go to court."

"Yeah, right there. And while I was up against the wall, my gull was coming from court. And when the police wasn't looking, we did our thang, ya hear me," I smiled.

Tez busted out laughing. "Ok, you did yo' thang, my nigga."

"Had to right there, ya hear me."

"Nigga you crazy. But forreal, though. I just hate that bitch ass shit."

"Errthang is errthang, bruh, ya hear me."

"So, what they say about you being on probation?"

"Oh yeah. I gotta go to court for that next. My lawyer said he was gone come and see me and let me know when I gotta go to court." I hadn't even realized I was standing up. I guess talking about the sneaky link me and my girl did got me all excited. I sat back down and look up at the ceiling, deep in thought about what to expect next.

"Did you ask yo' lawyers when you going back down the road?" asked Tez.

"My lawyer said it all depends on what Lauren Pedro wanna do. She can if she want to, but she might let me just sit in the county and kill it."

"Yeah, she can, but you know how these folks play. But you never know doe. She probably do let you kill it while you in the county."

I let out a sigh. "Yeah, she might.

"Damn, my nigga, I remember them days. Boy, when I was in this county fighting for my life seven years ago? Boy... forreal. I know we had this talk befo', and I notice you been going to prayer call and reading yo lil' Bible and stuff, lil' bruh. And I know you get tired of me talking about Allah, and I'm not trying to force you to believe what I believe, but God put you in this cell with me for a reason. And when I say God, I'm talking about Allah, fam. I'm finna go home off death row, fam. Thanks to Allah, lil' bruh. Forreal."

I narrowed my eyes at him, trying to keep my cool. "Tez, don't start with all this Malcolm X shit, ya hear me. Believe what you believe, and I stand on what I stand on. Just because I'm a Christian and you a Muslim don't mean we can't be cousins, my nigga, ya hear me."

Tez laughed. "I like that. You right, my nigga. I can't even argue witcha right there. You some' serious. Ian lyin', boy. That's why I mess witcha, my nigga, forreal."

"I already know you fuck with me," I said as I kicked off my shower shoes. "I'm finna get me some sleep, my nigga. I'll holla at cha later."

"Ok, that's wassup, my nigga. Just holla at me when you get up, fam."

Before he could even finish his sentence, I was already knocked out.

Probation Hearing

"How are you doing today, judge?" both of my lawyers said to Judge Pedro as she walked into the courtroom. Like the other judge, she was slim, had glasses, and had a no-nonsense attitude. My lawyers and I all stood there waiting on her—the woman who had the power to make our lives a living hell if she felt like it.

"Well, I'm doing good, Mr. Johnson and Mr. O'Kelly. Thanks for asking," she said tiredly as she took a seat. "You all may be seated," she added as she got settled in her chair.

"What do we have here today, Mr. Johnson and Mr. O'Kelly?"

Mr. Johnson cleared his throat. "Um, yes, Judge. Mr. Demario Jones here was placed on probation in your courtroom on October 31, 2010, for two years which he did really well on if you ask me, Judge. He had a job, he was reporting and paying his fines like he had been asked to do... but we are here today because he has caught a charge while on probation. But he has only 90 days left before he completes his probation term, so we would like to ask of you, honorable judge, that Mr. Jones probation not be revoked and let him finish his 90 days in the county jail or at least wait until the outcome of his case.

She flipped through the paperwork in front of her without looking up. "And what kind of case did Mr. Jones here catch while on probation, Mr. Johnson?"

"A capital offense, Judge," he admitted.

"Well, I'm sorry Mr. Johnson and Mr. O'Kelly, but Mr. Jones has caught a capital offense. It would be different if he had caught another burglary, but I'ma have to fully revoke his probation for now due to the fact Mr. Jones caught a capital offense while on probation."

Both of my lawyers took worried glances at each other. "Ok, thanks, Judge," said Mr. Johnson coldly.

They were upset, but I already knew the consequences before I went. So, hearing her verdict didn't really bother me. I knew I was either going to prison or staying in the county jail. Regardless, I was still going to be locked up and not going home.

"However, Mr. Johnson and Mr. O'Kelly," started Judge Pedro, "If Mr. Jones's case here comes back not void, then I will reinstate his probation."

"Okay, thank you, Judge," said Mr. Johnson.

"Sorry. Is there anything else I can do for y'all today? Mr. Johnson and Mr. O'Kelly?"

"Um, yes, Judge. Can me and Mr. O'Kelly go in the back and have a talk with Demario and his mother? If it's ok."

"Well, of course, Mr. Johnson. I don't have any problem with that.

"Thanks, Judge," said Mr. Johnson as me and my lawyers headed to the back. Inside was a long table with about five chairs on each side. There were black and white abstract pictures on the wall with hints of one accent color on each. Mama had on a black silk dress, kitten heels, and a silver necklace that I had bought for her a few months ago. Her hair was bone straight and rested right on her shoulders.

"Hey, how are you doing today, Miss Terry? Glad you made it here today," greeted Mr. Johnson as we sat down at the table.

"I'm doing fine, and you?" asked Mama.

"I guess I'm okay," laughed Mr. Johnson. He tried his best to lighten the mood and make us feel like everything was okay and under control. I knew the truth, though. He was just as uncertain about what was going to happen to me as the rest of us.

"Dat's good. Can I ask you something?" questioned Mama.

"Yes, ma'am. Go ahead."

"Okay, 'cuz I got here late, so I wanted to know since the judge revoke his probation, does that mean he have to go back to prison, or is he going to be able to stay here in the county jail?"

"Well, we was trying to get the judge to let him stay here in the county jail since he only got 90 days left on probation, but by the judge fully revoking his probation, that means he has to go back to prison and finish the rest of his probation time until the outcome of his case."

"And how much time is that? 90 days?" I couldn't help but sigh. *Mama, the man just told you I'm finna have to get on that bus and go down that road for some time, and you talking 'bout 90 days,* I thought to myself. Luckily, my lawyers were patient.

"Well, right now, he's backing up 8 years with no good time," said Mr. O'Kelly.

"Oh my God!" Mama cried. I hated seeing her like that.

"Man. I'm ready to go back upstairs," I said as I looked away from my momma. When I say seeing her like that tears me up... it really gets to me. I felt like she did it, hoping they would feel pity for me, but I knew the system didn't care about nothing but hanging my ass.

"Ok, we will let you go back upstairs in just a second. But, first, we need to know what all happened on this capital case before we leave today, so we can get this over with as fast as we can," assured Mr. O'Kelly.

"Mama, gone leave. I don't wanna talk to nobody, and I don't wanna talk to nobody 'bout nun," I responded as I stood up from the table.

"Okay. Love you, and make sure you call me later," said Mama as she wiped the tears from her eyes.

"Aite, ma. Bye. I love you too."

"Okay. Call me later," she whispered as she walked out of the visitor's room.

"So, are you going to tell us your side of the story or not, Demario?" Mr. O'Kelly asked me.

"Man, take me back to my cell," I snapped. I knew they meant well, but I was mad 'cuz it hurt me to see my momma crying and stressing all because of me and my lifestyle.

"Well, okay, have it your way from here on out," Mr. O'Kelly responded as he got up and walked out of the visitor's room.

"What's the matter, Demario? Are you okay?" Mr.

Johnson asked me as the door closed behind Mr. O'Kelly.

"Yeah, I'm good. I'm just ready to go back to my cell and lay down."

"What's bothering you, buddy?" he asked, clearly unconvinced with my initial answer. I just looked to the side as if I didn't hear him. "You can talk to me about anything anytime you need to. Ok?"

"Dats wassup. I just got a lot on my mind right now."

"Okay, well, I know you're probably upset because you gotta go back to prison and don't wanna go. But you gotta stay positive, buddy. Okay?"

"Aite, dats wassup. I hear ya."

"Alright. Come on, let's get out of here." He straightened his tie and pushed his seat away from the table. He patted my shoulder before we both walked out of the visitor's room and back into the courtroom.

"Are you done with Mr. Jones here, Bob? If so, I'll go ahead and take him back upstairs," the police asked my lawyer as I sat down in the courtroom.

"Um, yes, he's all good to go. Thanks."

"Alright, come on, Mr. Jones," the police said to me as I got up out of my seat and headed out the courtroom. To the 9th floor we go....

Back in My Cell

"Wassup, fam. What they do for you in court today?" Tez asked me as I walked back into my cell. He was playing with a piece of lint on the edge of his cover.

"Shit, Lauren Pedro dirty ass fully revoked a nigga," I shook my head.

"I knew she was gon' do that because you got that cap pending."

"I'm already hip. I rather be down the road anyway."

"I can feel that! Did you ask your lawyer about you having to go to Kilby lock-up when you get down the road?"

"Naw, I ain't even bring it up to them. I rather go down there and find out when I get down there."

"Oh, ok. Shit, you might not have to."

"Shit, I hope so, so I can gone get my G.E.D and me a lil' trade while I'm down there." If I was gonna be locked up, I might as well make the most of it. I heard of a few different people who learned how to do this and that in prison. Once they got out, even though they had records, they were still able to get a good-paying job. That restitution shit ain't no joke, and nothing's worse than being free but being scared that you gon' have to go back because you can't get a job to give them folks they money.

"Hell yeah. Dats what time it is," said Tez. "Shid… you might as well gone let me cut yo' hair now."

I chuckled. "Yeen lyin'. You know how to cut hair for-real?"

"I mean, I ain't the *best* barber in the world, but yo' shit can be decent."

"Dats wassup. When you gone be ready?"

"Shid… you got some razors? If you do, I'll cut it right now."

"Knawl, I don't have no razors."

Tez furrowed his eyebrow. "Hold on, I'm finna hit the button and ask the police do they got some in the cube out there." He got off the bed and hit the red button next to the cell door.

A few minutes later, a voice sounded over the intercom. "Yeah, wassup?" the police responded on the speaker in the cell.

"Yeah, I was just tryna see do y'all got some razors out there in the cube? 'Cuz I was trying to get some so I can cut my celly hair for him before he go down the road."

"Yeah, come on out and get 'em," the police said as he popped our cell door open. As Tez went out the cell, I sat on the bed thinking about how disappointed my gul was going to be when she found out I had to go back to prison. *Damn, Mario, you really got yourself into some bull shit,* I thought to myself.

"Let's get it, nigga, ain't no need for you to be looking crazy 'cuz yo' ass going down that road," Tez said to me as he came back in the cell shaking the razors.

I busted out laughing. Tez was a trip, but he was real. "Nigga, you crazy."

"Here you go, nigga, gone comb yo' hair out first," Tez laughed as he handed me a comb. I grabbed it and looked in the mirror as I started picking the knots out my hair.

"Damn, boy. I remember when I caught the chain the first time and had to cut my shit. I was mad as hell," Tez remembered as he looked at the wall.

"I'm already hip, but it's too late in the game to complain, ya hear me."

"Hell yeah," agreed Tez. "Wassup? you ready?"

"Yeah, let's do it," I grunted as I grabbed my blanket off the bed. I folded it up to sit on the toilet for some cushion to make myself more comfortable while Tez cut my hair.

"Damn, nigga, you got some good shit. I thought you had nigga hair like mine," Tez observed as he held the razor to my scalp. Slowly, he began cutting my hair with a comb and a razor jail house style. We didn't have any clippers, so we had to work with what we had.

"I told you my momma white and my daddy Mexican," I smirked.

"Nigga, yo' shit ain't that good," he laughed. "Nigga sit still foe I fuck around and cut yo' ass with this razor why you playin'."

"Aite, my nigga, come on," I responded as I straightened up.

"On some real shit doe, my nigga, I hate you gotta go back down that road."

"It is what is. I'ma be aite, ya hear me."

"I know you ain't trippin' on going back down the road. I'm talking about yo' case, my nigga."

"That shit crazy, ain't it bruh?" I sighed.

"Hell yeah, my nigga. I remember like yesterday when them folks gave me the death penalty and sent me down the road to Kilby lock-up."

"Like what was going through yo head when you heard the judge say 'death penalty?'" I asked.

"Talkin' bout when he sentenced me in the courtroom to the death penalty?"

"Yeah."

"Dog, that's the worst feeling in the world. If I had to go to court on a nigga who kilt my momma and everybody I love, I still wouldn't wish that shit on a nigga, dog."

"Damn." I can only imagine. It's bad enough knowing that once they say you guilty, that you guilty. It's another thing for them to say not only are you guilty, but you have to *die* too for what you did. That shit is wild.

"Why you think I be on you like I do? 'Cuz I been where you at, so I feel ya pain, my nigga." Tez took a step back and looked at my head. "I got it cut down low as I can get it with the razor, lil bruh. How you want it? Low and even all over or what?" he asked.

"Yeah, low and even all over 'cuz they gon' clean me out again when I get down the road anyway."

"Aite. Bet," said Tez as he started back cutting my hair.

"Look at all my hair on the floor," I mumbled as I looked at the floor in the cell. "Dat shit crazy."

"Dat shit ah grow back, nigga."

"I'm already hip," I said as I touched my freshly cut hair.

A Month Later

"Jones? Demario Jones?" the police yelled on the speaker in the cell, trying to wake me up.

"Yeah," I responded as I rubbed the sleep out of my eyes.

"Pack up all your stuff that you taking with you and come out to the cube. You're on the chain this morning," the police officer said as he popped my cell door open. This one was white, beefy, and had brown hair and a clean-shaven face.

"Aite. Dats wassup. Let me get myself together. I'm on my way," I said sleepily as I got up and put my shower sliders on.

"Alright, buddy. Waiting on you," the police said smoothly.

I grabbed my toothbrush and toothpaste from off the table as I heard Tez turn around in his bed to face me.

"You gone, ain't it, my nigga?" he asked as he let out a big yawn.

"Hell yeah," I sighed as I brushed my teeth. "I'm gone, my nigga."

"Dats wassup, fam. Keep ya head up, lil' bruh. Stay the same."

"You already know." I finished brushing my teeth and grabbed my face rag off the table to wash up. "You too," I added as I dapped him up after I finished at the sink. With one last look around, I grabbed all my stuff and walked out the cell to the cube.

"Alright, Jones. You ready?" the police asked me as I made it to the cube. He was sipping coffee looking at the newspaper while the other officer with him was playing on his phone

"Yeah, I'm ready."

"Okay. Make sure you got everything 'cuz once we get downstairs, ain't no coming back up here."

"I got errthang," I responded.

"Alright then. Let's head out, buddy." Just like that, I was on my way back to prison for the second time at 23 years old, facing the death penalty. A nigga was feeling real sick.

Back in the Joint

"Alright! Everybody off the bus and straight between those gates right there. And up against the wall, so I can get the handcuffs and shackles off y'all," the police said as he opened the doors.

"Now. I'ma give y'all a chance right now to throw anything you don't suppose to have in your possession right here in this white bucket," the Correctional Officer said as he came out the back door. He was a black guy, maybe a good 6 foot, and looked like he probaly played a sport at some point in his past. The pepper-spray on his waist jiggled every time he spoke.

"So don't nun of y'all have no cell phones, dope, knives, or any kind of weapon or anything you gotta ask yourself do I suppose to have," he continued. "If so, I'm finna go back inside for a second, so that give y'all time enough to throw all y'all contraband in this bucket right here now. However, if we shake you down and find anything you don't suppose to have, we gon' beat cho ass and throw you in lock-up and let you stay back there until you heal up. Now, do everybody understand?"

Damn, a nigga back in this shit again, I thought to myself. What was I thinking?

"Alright. They are all yours," the police said to the Correctional Officer as he finished taking all the handcuffs and shackles off us and handing him some papers.

"Alright. See you next week," the Correctional Officer responded as he grabbed the papers from the police and went back into the building.

"Alright. Y'all gone do ya time and come on home," the police said to us as he went out the back gate, got back on the bus, and pulled off.

A few moments later, the C.O. came back out of the building. "Everybody must be clean and don't have nothing they don't suppose to 'cuz I don't see nothing inside my bucket," he said as he looked in the white bucket. "Alright, everybody grab your property and go in through that door right there. Stand in one of those black squares on the floor in there and set your property down in front of you so we can go through all y'all stuff."

So, we all grabbed our belongings and did what we were told. "Now, I don't know who it is, but I been doing this 20+ years, and it never fail. It's always one stupid motha fucka out the bunch who try to be slick, and we catch they ass every time," the C.O said as he and several others came in behind us and started going through our property. While they were looking through our things, we stood up against the wall and watched them violate our privacy.

"I guess it's true what they say. It's a first time for everythang," the C.O. said once they finished searching our personal property. "I'm surprised that nobody had nothing they were not supposed to have. Everybody grab your property and follow me so we can get y'all processed and in the system." We quickly followed suit behind him to the process section. All types of new inmates were joining me in this hell. White, black, Mexicans...you name it. Some of the dudes looked nervous, probably 'cuz it's their first time here. A few of them looked sad because it was their second time here. I was definitely one of them. A few of them looked scared because they thought prison would be like it is in the movies. Lastly, you got the dudes who act like they're *glad* to be here. I don't know what the fuck *they* got going on.

"Alright, I have a card with everybody's name on it," said the C.O. as we all stood on the squares on the floor. "When you hear your name called, come up front, get your card, and fill it out." He looked one of the bigger guys up and down. "If you can't read or write," he continued, "come up front so I can help you fill it out." No one moved a muscle. "So, everybody can read and write? Good. Now make sure y'all put the correct shoe size and correct pants and shirt size and T-shirt and boxers, so we will have y'all bags ready by the time y'all get through showering. Do everybody understand? If not, raise ya hand."

Again, nobody moved a muscle. We all just stood there looking like we were ready to go. "Alright, let's get started," said the C.O. "When you hear your name called, come up front and get your card and a pen from out this box and fill it out. After y'all fill them cards out, get back on your square until everybody is done with they card." As they called each name, all I could do was pray. Pray that I wouldn't have to go to lock-up. *As long as I don't have to go to lock-up, I can make it through all this*, I thought to myself. The whole check-in process took about 10 minutes.

"Now the next thang I'ma do is call y'all up here one by one so you can tell me your charge and your date of birth and social security number, so we can make sure it matches what we have on record. And once we get through with this process, y'all can start taking y'all showers. Do everybody understand what I just said? If not, raise ya hand." Again. Straight crickets. *I wish we can hurry this shit up*, I thought to myself.

"Alright let's get started," said the C.O. as he begin calling names. As I stood there on the square waiting for my name to be called, I started thanking God in my head that I didn't have to go to lock-up.

2nd Day in Population

Clink! Clink! Clink! was the sound of the Correctional Officer's knight stick hitting the iron frame of my bed as he was trying to wake me up out of my sleep.

"Yeah," I responded as I woke up and pulled my blanket from over my head. I could still feel the crust in my eyes when I noticed several Correctional Officers standing around my bed.

"What's your name and A.I.S number?" asked the Correctional Officer. This was one was musty and had some bad breath. He must've been in a rush to get to work.

"Demario Jones. 267787.

"Alright. Jump down for me and put your shoes on."

Quickly, I rolled out of the bed and put on my shoes like I was told. *The fuck they want?* I wondered as I stood up and looked at the officer who was doing the talking.

"Alright, put all your property that belongs to you in this bag right here for me," the C.O. said as he handed me a bag. "Now turn around and put your hands behind your back." Like a zombie, I turned around and put my hands behind me. One of the other C.O.s put handcuffs on me while another put shackles around my ankles. Once they were done, the main one looked at me again.

"Alright, this way," he said as he grabbed me by the arm on one side while another officer did the same on the other. The two walked me out of the dorm along with the rest of the C.O.s like I was a madman who was hard to tame. *Y'all really do the fucking most,* I thought to myself. Just because I'm in here doesn't mean I'm stupid. All this security and me with no weapon or nothing, do they really think I would try and fight back or something if just one of them came in there with me?

"Hold up right here," one of the C.Os said to me as we got ready to exit the dorm. I stood in the doorway, looking down at my feet and trying to process what was going on. I was sleeping so damn good before they came in there fucking with me....

"Alright. Everybody on the hallway turnaround and face the wall. Deadman walkin' in!" he yelled to all the inmates walking in the hallway as they turned to face the wall.

"Aye man, get cho stupid ass up against the got damn wall," hissed another C.O. I stood there thinking 'bout my first time in the joint when I was the one facing the wall. You could've never told me then that I'd be back in prison as the deadman walkin'.

"Damn," I said to myself as I shook my head.

"When we walk up this hall, if I catch any one of y'all looking back at this man, I'ma beat cho ass," the C.O. said to the inmates as the other officers grabbed me on both sides and begin walking me up the hallway to the main lock-up gate entrance.

"Pop the gate!" the C.O. said on his radio as we pulled up to the front gate of lock-up. When the gate came open, we all walked inside. "Stop right here. Let me take these shackles off for ya," the C.O. said to me as we entered lock-up. "What cell you got Demario Jones going to?" he asked the lieutenant as he finished taking the shackles off me.

"Um... 23 cell on the backside on the bottom," he responded uninterested. He was more caught up in what was going on on his phone than on me.

"Ok." The two C.O.s grabbed me and walked me to my cell. "Roll 23 cell on the backside on the bottom open for me," one of the C.O.'s said on his radio as we pulled up to the empty cell. When the door opened, the C.O. walked in, set my bag with my property on the bed, then came back out. "Alright, gone in the cell," he said to me as I walked inside, still in handcuffs.

"Aite. Roll 23 cell on the bottom back lock for me on the backside." The cell door squeaked as it rolled back shut. "Alright. Come to the tray hole, so I can get them handcuffs off ya," the C.O. instructed.

Once the C.O. removed the handcuffs, he walked away from the cell. I looked around at my new home. It was smaller than the cell I was in before with Tez. The bed was small and looked uncomfortable. Sigh. This was my new life.

"Oh, now 23 cell. Wassup?" a deep raspy voice said from the shadows. It was an inmate calling my cell number, trying to get my attention. He sounded a lot like Samuel L. Jackson.

"Yeah, wassup?" I responded flatly.

"Nun. Just hollin' at cha. They call me Dec, my nigga."

"Dats wassup. They call me Yo."

"You said Yo?"

"Yeah, Yo."

"Dats wassup, my nigga."

"Say, Dec. You know 'round what time it is?"

"Yeah. It's 1:33 a.m."

Damn. I wonder why they decided to move me in the middle of the damn night like that. "Dats wassup. I'll chop it up witcha when I get up. Let me get myself together."

"Aite, dats wassup, Bruh Bruh. Do your thang."

With that, I began unpacking my stuff from out the bag so I could make up my bed and lay down. As I looked around the cell, I couldn't help but trip on how small the cell was. The toilet was inches from the head of the bed and the cell itself was dark and cold.

I know it was prison but damn. This was worse than being in a damn dungeon. I took my sheets and blanket out my bag and set them on the bed. I was tired as hell and ready to go back to bed. Slowly, I set my bag on the table and began making my bed as fast as I could so I could lay down and warm myself up. Once I got through making my bed, I jumped straight in it and went to sleep.

***

"Chow call! Chow call!" the C.O. yelled at me from my cell door, trying to wake me up.

"Yeah," I mumbled as I woke up and noticed him standing at the cell door with a tray in his hand.

"Got damn, man. You sleep hard as hell," the C.O. said irritatedly as he set the food in the tray hole and walked away. I got up from the bed and grab my tray. Fruit cup, "chicken" patty, and a piece of bread. I wasn't really in the mood to eat, so I set it on the table and laid back down to go back to sleep.

"Pill call," the nurse said as she pulled up to my door to get my medication from my hand. "Good morning, Mr. Jones," she sang as she gave me my meds through the tray hole. I was taking pain pills for my hand.

"Morning," I said in a sleepy voice. "How you doing?"

"I'm fine," she said sweetly. I bet she one of them ladies who makes cookies for her grandkids. I just got that vibe from her just by hearing her voice. "You have a nice day now," she said as she walked off from my cell.

"Aite you too," I responded as I snatched my cup off the table to get some water. After knocking those two pills back, I climbed back into the bed and went back to sleep.

***

"Chow call! Chow call!" the C.O. yelled as he shook the bards, trying to wake me up for lunch.

"I'm up," I said as I rolled over in my bed and grabbed the lunch tray. As I started eating my food, I looked around my cell for the first time during the day. My breakfast was still on the table from this morning.

"Oh, now Yo," Dec called me from next door.

"Yeah, wassup?" I said in a monotone voice.

"Come to the bars on the left side of yo' cell by the door, so I can ask you some real quick."

"Aite, give me a second. I'm eatin' right now, Dec, ya hear me." I shoved another forkful of cold vegetables into my mouth.

"Aite. Just holla at me when you get through eating." He paused for a second. "I see now yeen no people person."

"Why you say dat?" I asked.

"Cuz every time I try to holla at you, you brush me off."

I smacked my teeth. "Nigga, you trippin'. I just got up, dats all that is, ya hear me."

I heard him let out a breath. "Oh ok, my nigga. Just tryna fuck with my neighbor since we gotta sleep by each other, anyway, ya feel me?"

"Yeah, I hear ya," I said as I got up off the bed. *I need to clean up some,* I thought to myself. *I ain't no dirty ass dude.* After wiping off my mouth, I set my tray in the tray hole, grabbed my breakfast tray off the table, and slid it under the door.

"Dats wassup," continued Dec. "I just know how niggas think, but we basically live with each other. So, we may as well get along, my nigga. Feel me?"

"I'm already hip. I been doing time since a kid, so I'm already hip. It's just when I came in last night, I was tired, so I went straight to sleep. Then when I first wake up, I have to let my laptop load up a lil' longer than other people, ya hear me," I added as I washed my hands over the sink.

"Oh ok. I see what you saying."

"But wassup, Dec? I'm through eatin', ya hear me."

"Put yo' head to the bars, bruh. Do you see that?" Dec asked as he waved his hand back and forth with a piece of paper in his hand.

"Yeah, I see it."

"Grab it out of my hand."

"Aite," I said as I grabbed the piece of paper. When I opened it up, I noticed two rolling papers and some tobacco. Was I fucking dreaming?

"You smoke, don't it?" asked Dec.

"Hell yeah, I smoke!" I said hardly containing my excitement.

Dec busted out laughing. "That's all you, my nigga."

Now this is the kinda welcome I'm talking about, I thought to myself. Without hesitation, I started rolling up the cigarette so I could get my fill for the nicotine. "Dats wassup. 'Preciate it, Bruh. You got some fi."

"Yeah, here you go," said Dec as he passed me a wick.

I lit my cigarette and closed my eyes as I let the smoke fill my lungs. It had been months since I had a cigarette. The feeling almost had me lightheaded.

"If you don't mind me asking, what they got you in lock-up for?" queried Dec.

"Cuz I caught a capital murder case while I was on probation." I exhaled some more of the smoke.

"You know they put you in lock-up until the outcome of yo' case when you on probation like that."

"I'm already hip," I said as I flicked the cigarette in the toilet and sat down on the bed. I was in a daze when I heard another voice further down the hall.

"Oh now, Dec, I gotta scribe coming down the wall to

ya," the voice said to my "neighbor." Come to find out, the new voice belonged to a guy named Cody, who slept next door on the other side of my cell.

"Alright, Yo," Cody said to get my attention.

"Yeah? Wassup?" I responded as I got up off the bed and noticed Cody waving a piece of paper back and forth on the right side of my cell.

"Will you pass it to Dec?" he asked as I grabbed it from his hand.

"Preciate it, Yo," said Dec as he grabbed the note from me.

"You good," I responded as I sat back down on the bed. It's crazy how life can change at an instant. A year ago, I never thought I'd be talking to people I can't even see from a cell.

"When did you come to lock-up?" asked Cody, breaking my thoughts.

"Last night."

"How many days did they give you back here?"

"I'm back here on a probation violation."

"Dang, bro. I hate to hear that."

"Errthang good," I sighed. "But check this out. I'm finna lay back for a second, bruh, ya hear me."

"Aite, dats wassup, bruh."

I began looking through my property for my Daily Bread, and I couldn't find it. *I could've sworn I had it in here somewhere...* I thought to myself. My Daily Bread was basically a way for me to get more familiar with the Bible and God's teaching. I liked reading it, and it helped pass the time for sure.

I asked Cody did he have one. Luckily, he did and didn't mind sharing. After I grabbed it from him, I couldn't help but notice how different it was from the one I was used to.

"What kind of Daily Bread this is?" I asked Cody.

"That's a Daily Bread by Kenneth and Gloria Copeland call Faith to Faith."

"Aite, dats wassup. 'Preciate it. I'll give it back to ya when I get through reading the word for today."

"You good, go ahead and keep it, Yo. I just use it for the blank sheets of paper in the back of it to roll my cigarette when I don't have any rolling papers."

"Oh ok, dats wassup. I need it too." I wasn't about to let good material get put to waste like that. I sat down on the bed, opened the Daily Bread, and began reading the work for the day.

"Oh, now 23 cell!" somebody said in the shadows to get my attention.

"Yeah, wassup? Who that," I responded.

"This Scurry down here in 21 cell," the voice responded. Hold up. I know a nigga name Scurry...

"You talkin' 'bout Big Scurry from Birmingham who was in the county with me in '08 and '09?" I asked as I put the Daily Bread beside me on the bed.

"Yeah, nigga."

"Wassup, my nigga, you good?" I was glad to hear from somebody I know. Especially considering the circumstances.

"Yeah, I'm good. I thought you would've been at the house by now."

"I did go to the house, Scurry, but I fuck around and caught a cap case 90 days befo' I was finna get off probation. And that's how I end up back."

"Damn, Yo. I hate to hear that. Yeen got nobody on the case with you, do it?"

"Yea, I got one nigga on the case with me."

I heard Scurry let out a deep breath. "Damn, is the nigga keeping it solid witcha or what, Yo?"

"No comment, ya hear me," I said through gritted teeth. "But errthang gon' be straight. So how much time they end up giving you on yo cap anyway, Scurry?"

"Man, God blessed me, my nigga. I gotta 20 split 3 and a 20 split 4.

"Hell yeah, 7 years? Shidddd you should be home soon then."

"Yeah, next month on the 23rd."

"I'm already hip. Dats wassup, my nigga, on sum."

"Yo, what kinda case you had yo' first time in the county?"

"A burglary 1st."

"Oh ok, I thought you had an attempted murder case."

"Knawl, I had a burglary 1st," I responded. "So, can we catch store back here, Scurry?"

"Yeah, once a month."

I paused in shock. "Damn, so how much the limit is on the store?"

"$75."

"Damn, forreal?" What the fuck was I supposed to do with that?

"Yeah, then $25 of them gotta be hygiene and the rest for food."

Damn! They really out here robbing folks like that? "Straight up? Dats cold, bruh. Forreal…" I shook my head.

"Yeah, Yo. You done got yourself in some real deep shit this time," laughed Scurry.

"Yeen lying, so when do we put the store slips in to catch the store?"

"They pass them out the first Tuesday of every month, and we catch the store the day after on Wednesday."

"Aite, dats wassup. So, we can catch the store the first Wednesday of err month?"

"Yeah."

"So, that mean we catch the store next week then?"

"Yeah."

"Dats wassup. So ain't no phones back here? I need to call my momma and see if she put that money on my books for me yet."

"Yeah, it's some back here, but niggas be playing games back here in these cells. So, niggas don't be too quick to let niggas use they phone. But I can shoot a text for ya."

"Aite, bet." Something is always better than nothing.

"Just write what you want me to text yo Mama and the phone number down on the scribe. Then send it down here to me."

"Aite, I'm finna write the scribe now. You gotta pen down there I can use?" I asked.

"Yeah, I'm finna send it down the wall to Cody now," said Scurry. A few moments later, Cody was passing me a black ink pen.

"Aite, 'preciate it, bruh," I said as I grabbed the pen from Cody and began writing the note for Scurry to text my momma for me.

```
Hey Ma. I'm okay. Please don't forget
    the money if you can. Love You.


              Demario
```

"Yo, you ain't have you no kids while you was out there?" asked Scurry.

"Hell naw," I responded, trying to concentrate on what I was writing.

"You must can't have children?"

"Yeah, I can have children." The fuck kinda question is that?

"So, you was out there all that time, and ain't nobody come up pregnant?"

"Yeah, but I gotta abortion."

"Why you had an abortion?"

"Cuz I wanna be there for my kids, my nigga," I admitted. "I don't wanna be in and out of they life. I rather not even put them through this shit until I'm out the streets and got my life together, ya feel me."

"Yeah, I guess so, Yo," Scurry said unconvinced.

"I'm finna pass this scribe down the wall to Cody now," I said as I finished writing the note. "Oh, now Cody, when do they take us outside for our walk?" I asked.

"Man, bruh, they ain't took us outside since I been back here, and I been back here damn near a month!"

What in the whole....a month? That's the shit they on in lock-up? "Forreal?" I gasped. I was legit stunned.

"Hell yeah. They handle us. Fuck up on that walk, bruh, forreal."

"Damn, so how long do we supposed to go outside every day anyway?" I asked, still trying to get past the fact that this man hasn't felt the sun in over a month.

"We supposed to go outside an hour every day."

"And you say you been back here damn near a month and ain't went outside period?"

"Hell yeah, bruh. Not one time."

"Dats crazy how these folks handle a nigga forreal."

"I already know, bruh."

"That's why I'm so mad with myself for coming back to this shit, bruh, forreal," I said as I balled up my fist. I just knew I was more than this situation that I was in...

"Oh now, Yo, I gotta scribe coming down the wall to you, bruh," interrupted Scurry.

"Aite, come on with it," I said briskly as Cody handed me the scribe. The note said that my momma put some on my books and she loved me. "Aite, dats wassup. 'Preciate it, Scurry."

"One thang 'bout momma... she gon' come through for a nigga ain't it, Yo?" asked Scurry.

"Hell yeah. I might have to wait 'til she get paid, but she gon' come through for me every time," I said proudly.

Scurry clicked his tongue. "Hell yeah, when them hoes get gone on a nigga and them bitch-ass niggas... momma gone hold a nigga down ain't it, man?"

"Hell yeah," I agreed.

"Man, Yo. You gotta come from under that shit, dog. Forreal, don't let them folks give you no thousand years in that courtroom."

"I'm already hip, my nigga. I been doing everything in my power to keep my mind off that shit. That's why I stay in that Bible 'cuz dats the only thang that bring me peace, my nigga. Forreal."

"Oh, I already know what you going through, my nigga. Just stay prayed up and keep reading that Bible and be forreal with God, and you gon' be straight. We gotta homeboy name Big Ben who be having prayer call back here every night, and we gotta another homeboy name Bruh Lacey who do it too."

"Oh, they be having prayer call back here in the cells?" I asked. They couldn't do anything else right, so it's hard to believe they would even do *that*.

"Yeah, every night at 9:00."

"Oh okay, dats wassup. And how long it last 'bout a hour or some?" I asked.

"Naw, it don't be nothing but like 10, 15, or 20 minutes. It depend on who do it. Then I forgot they just move Big Ben to the other side a couple of days ago anyway. So, Bruh Lacey da only one on this side who do it anyway, and he usually in and out of there in 10 or 15 minutes."

"Dats wassup," I said as I thought about the prayer call I was going to at the other spot. It would be a lot different with not being able to see him, but hey. A word is a word, right?

"Yeah, I listen to it every night," sighed Scurry. "It be good too. I be needing to hear that word."

"Nigga, you wasn't going to church on the streets," said Scurry.. "Now them folks tryna give yo' ass all that time. Now you wanna spend some time with God."

That made me bust out laughing. I guess he did have a point. When I was in the streets, church was the *last* thing on my mind.

"Man, nigga you crazy," I chuckled.

"But I know on some real shit, Yo," started Scurry. "A lot of times, God sit us down and put us in situations like this to teach us some. Was you going to church while you was out there on the streets?"

"Yeah. I went a couple of times while I was out there."

"So, you telling me you woke up Sunday morning and went to church by yoself?" Scurry asked, sounding surprised.

"Yeah, me and my gul, and her folks."

"Oh ok, so you had a gul when you left the streets. Has she been fuckin' witcha since you been locked up?"

"She locked up right now, too," I sighed.

"Oh, she locked up too? What they lock yo gul up for?"

"While the police was searching the house, they found some heroin in her purse." I shook my head in the darkness as I thought back to that day. I still don't even know why she had that shit in the first place.

"Damn, what the fuck she was doing with some heroin in her purse?" questioned Scurry, reading my mind.

"Yo' guess is as good as mine, Scurry, ya hear me."

"Yeah, I heard you loud and clear. Sound like yo' gul was a smoker," Scurry laughed. "But how much she had in her purse, Yo?"

That's a good question. I didn't really have a clue. "I can't even tell ya. I just know they found some in there. I was just ready to go to jail and go to sleep, my nigga."

"I'm hip. I know how a nigga be feeling when them folks hit a nigga with that capital murder shit."

"Hell yeah. Scurry, yeen got no pain pills down there?" I asked as I flexed my hand. "Damn. I need me some. My hand hurtin' like a mothafucka. "

"What happen to yo' hand?" Scurry asked.

Then I went on to tell him about how I got shot while I was catching the case and how the nurses were only giving me two pain pills a day.

When I finished, Scurry started laughing. "Well, gotta thank God a nigga still alive, ain't it, man?" said Scurry.

"Scurry, it seem like yesterday we was in the county jail together, sweatin' to go home. Now, you finna get out, and I'm back in this bitch," I sighed.

"Hell yeah. I got 30 more days and this shit ova."

"After 7 years, I know you ready to get out this shit."

"Hell yeah, my nigga, forreal. This shit ain't for me, my nigga. Dats why I'ma do my best to stay out the way when I get out there."

"Got to, Scurry. 'Cuz this ain't no way for a nigga to live. Forreal. Look how they got us back here in these lil' ass cells with the toilet right by a nigga head, and you can't flush the toilet but one time in a hour," I started to get mad again just thinking about the shit. "But they say innocent until proven guilty. I can't tell though... Got me in a cell 24 hours a day. These hoes crazy."

"Bruh, it's niggas who done came back here off death row and said it's worser back here than it is on death row!"

Out of nowhere, something shot past my cell super-fast. It almost looked like a bird but it was small and white. "Man, what the fuck that was dat just flew past my cell like that?" I shouted.

Scurry laughed. "That's what they call a horseback here. It's a string tied to a sock. That's how niggas get shit from cell to cell back here. Just in case somebody sleep down the wall, and you can't pass yo' scribe or get a wick or cigarette or whatever, that's what niggas use to pass shit to each other."

I swear niggas always find a way to do some shit. I had to give credit where it was due. "Oh ok. Yeah, dat shit smart." Man, what kind of place did they send me to?

"This shit crazy as hell back here, ain't it, man?" Scurry laughed. "Nigga, you ain't gone lose your mind back here is it, Yo?"

"Hell naw. This shit can't break no nigga like me. My mind too strong."

"Chow! Chow call! Chow call!" the runner yelled to let us know it was time to eat.

"Damn, what time it is?" I asked Scurry. I couldn't believe it was time to eat already.

"Shid 'bout 3 or 3:30."

Wait.....what? That don't sound right... "And we eatin' dinner this early? So what about the rest of the night?"

"Shidddd we dead 'til breakfast after this, Yo."

"Man, this shit real. Forreal," I laughed nervously. "So, basically what they telling a nigga... after this. Take a shower and go to bed."

"Hell naw. We took our shower yesterday, and we don't take showers back here but every other day. So, we dead on the showers until tomorrow."

Was I hearing things? "Man... you lying."

"No, I ain't. On errthang," said Scurry.

"Chow call! Chow call!" said the C.O. as he pulled up to my cell and set my dinner in the tray hole.

Hell yeah, a nigga hungry as hell, I thought to myself as

I snatched my food out the tray hole. When I took the lid off my tray, I noticed a meat patty, some mashed potatoes, some beans, and a piece of cornbread. *Man... look at this shit,* I thought as I got back off the bed to set the tray back in the tray hole. "Man, what the fuck I did to deserve this shit here," I said to myself as I sat back down on the bed, confused and mad about being back in the joint.

"How you like that meat patty, nigga?" Scurry asked me, being funny.

I chuckled. "You already know." We both knew that shit was trash. "Man, I gotta do some with my life. I can't keep coming back to this shit, bruh. Forreal."

"Yeen lying, my nigga. Dats all I be ova here thinking 'bout. How I'ma stay out this bitch, my nigga."

"Hell yeah. I need to sign up for my G.E.D. while I'm back here. Who I need to holla at to do that, Scurry?"

"Oh, they don't let you take nun while you back here. You gotta wait until you through with yo' case first."

Damn, was he forreal? A nigga can't even better himself while he locked up?

"Nigga, on God these folks consider us a dead man walking back here, forreal," said Scurry as he answered my thoughts. "You see what they make everybody do when you walkin' down the hallway in handcuffs and shackles. Turn around and face the wall."

I heard someone shift in their cell. You would think people would be talking more at 3 in the afternoon. Nope. Apart from Scurry and me talking, it was pretty quiet.

"Did the police holla out dead man walking when they brought you to lock-up coming down that hallway?" asked Scurry.

"Hell yeah."

"Aite then, you guilty already, and we ain't nothing in they eyes, bruh. See, they stuck a nigga in these lil' ass cells with these big ass roaches and big ass rats running through this bitch at night time, and I know you felt how cold it was in this bitch last night. So what that tell you about these folks?"

"They don't give a fuck about no nigga."

"Exactly."

I let out a deep sigh. Then something Scurry said stuck out in my mind. "It be rats back in this bitch, doe?"

"Hell yeah!" laughed Scurry.

"Oh, hell nah. I don't fuck with rats. Period." I ain't ever been a nigga that fuck with any kind of rodents forreal. I might have grown up near the hood, but we didn't deal with no dirty shit like that. Just the thought of it made me shiver a little bit.

"See, Yo, these rats don't give a damn if you fuck with them or not. They still pullin' up, fuckin' with a nigga late night," pressed Scurry.

"Man, you playing."

"Nigga, on God! Then when it get hot, it be snakes and everything back in this bitch! Then it get so hot back here in these cells in the summertime, the folks have to come back here and spray the cells down with the hose pipes to cool the cell down."

"On God, he ain't lying, Yo," Dec agreed.

"Damn, this shit the jungle forreal," I sighed.

"Oh yeah, Yo," continued Scurry, "Remind me to tell the runner to brang you some extra blankets 'cuz it's gon' get so cold tonight you gon' have to block yo' cell door off to keep that cold ass air from coming in yo' cell."

"Aite, dats wassup. 'Preciate it, my nigga."

"Aite, I'ma tell him when he come to pick the trays up," promised Scurry. "But Yo, on some real shit, dog, this shit serious. These folks tryna give you the death penalty, bruh. And I know how you feel 'cuz I went through that same shit. The only way I got blessed with them two split is God, lil bruh. Forreal. Just like I was telling you, my nigga, God got you back here to get yo' attention, and He trying to show you some'. He knew it was gon' take for you to be over there in that cell by yourself to teach you what He tryna teach you. Because when you was on the streets, you had too much going on to da point God couldn't get yo' attention."

"On some real shit, Scurry, these folks got a nigga facing all of it right here, so a nigga can laugh or crash, ya hear me," I chuckled. "But on some real shit, Scurry, it's crazy you said dat 'cuz I been hearing that since I been lock-up this time."

"Hearing what?"

"God tryna get my attention. I'm already hip, though. I remember when my grandma used to tell me when God want you, you can't run." Gotta love Granny, man. She always gave me words of wisdom, even when I wasn't looking for it. I can still remember coming to her house to get a plate of homemade smothered porkchops, mashed potatoes, and collard greens on any given Sunday. While I'd be grubbing, she would be telling me different stories about her life and trying to just tell me what's what about these streets. I'd give anything to see her right about now...

"Hell nall, you can't," said Scurry, interrupting my thoughts.

"Yeah, ever since I been locked up this time on this bid right here, all I been around is somebody telling me about God. And the crazy thang is ever since this old school nigga named Sam started teaching me about the Bible, I really like to read it like every day."

"See, Yo, you probably done heard it befo', but you was so blind and stuck on the thangs of the world and so used to doing thangs the way you wanted to that you didn't understand or care about what you was hearing. So you didn't really pay it no attention like that, and God knew it was gon' take for you to be in a situation like you in for you to understand what He tryna show you. But, Yo, I just told the runner to brang you some blankets down there to yo' cell."

"Aite. 'Preciate it, bruh."

"So, Yo, when you got back out there, was it hard?"

"Man, I got out that bitch thinking I was finna go stay with my momma and get me a lil' job and stack me some money for 'bout six months rent-free until I could get on my feet and get my own spot and car. But my momma said I couldn't stay with her, so then I went to my pop's house and was staying with him until he got drunk one night and went to tripping on a nigga. I was staying with him for 'bout a week before he was tryna fight on that drunk shit. So, I dipped from that nigga house and went ova my homegul Red house and started staying with her for a while. She let a nigga stay there rent-free, and she was feeding a nigga for 'bout two months, and nobody would hire no nigga on a job. So… I jump back in the streets headfirst and ended up back in this bitch in this lil' ass cell."

"Damn so why yo momma wouldn't let you stay with her?" questioned Scurry.

"I ain't stayed with my momma since I was 15, Scurry, but I thought since I had went to prison, she would let a nigga come home and stay with her until I get on my feet. But shid…" my voice trailed off. It was actually complicated. I love Ma, but you know how it is when you young and think you know everything. Pretty much, without me tellin' too much to Scurry… she wasn't having that shit I was on.

"That ain't what I asked you," probed Scurry. "I said why yo' momma ain't let you stay with her?"

"All the fucked up shit I did growing up. Nun major doe. Just being a lil' nigga, dat's all."

"Oh ok. So who you stayed with when she put you out at 15?"

"Momma Nene and Auntie Bird."

"Oh, some mo' of yo' folks?"

"Knawl, dat's my partna momma and auntie. I just call his momma, Momma Nene, and his auntie, Auntie Bird." Momma Nene and Auntie Bird was looking out for me for years. Every time I got kicked out or just needed a quick place to crash, they always opened their doors up to me.

"Oh ok, and they wasn't tripping about you staying with them?"

"Hell knawl. Momma Nene and Auntie Bird cool as hell. On sum."

"Oh ok, so why yo' daddy was trippin'?"

"Dats just how he is when he get drunk. He been like dat since I was a lil' nigga."

"Oh, so he just was on some drunk shit one night and went to trippin', so you dipped?"

"Hell yeah. Nigga ain't got time for that shit. I just got out too, shid. A nigga was tryna stay OUT of prison."

"Ain't no way I'll handle my son like that fresh out the joint," said Scurry.

"Right. When I was young, I stole some money from my grandma, and my daddy still holding a grudge on a nigga 'bout dat shit. Dats just how he is."

"How much money you stole anyway?"

"They say I stole $1,000."

"$1,000? And how old you was?"

"Hmm... 'bout 9 or 10." I heard a few gasps from the cell around me.

"What the hell you did with $1,000 at 10 years old, Yo?"

"Fuck it up at the candy man house and at this lil' food spot by the library we used to walk to after school every day."

"So you spent $1,000 at the candy lady house?"

"Not all of it. My momma caught me with about $700 of the money after school one day at the library when she picked me and my sisters up after school one day."

"What yo' momma said when she found the money?"

"She asked me where I get the money from, and I told her I found it in the alley on the way from school."

"And yo momma believe that shit?"

"Yeah, until two months later when my grandma noticed the money was gone."

"Damn. It took yo' grandma two months befo' she noticed the money was gone?"

"Hell yeah. She had so much money in her drawer on the dresser when I first seen it, I thought it was just regular paper."

"Damn. I wonder why she ain't have it in the bank..." Scurry's voice drifted off like he was in deep thought.

"Shidddd me too, but I know one thang. It done got cold as hell back here. Where dat runner at with them blankets, Scurry?"

"Damn, Yo, you should've been said sum when he came and pick them trays up. It's too late now; he gone for the night."

I let out a frustrated groan as I looked into the darkness. "Damn, my nigga gon' fuck around and freeze back in this bitch," I said in a cold voice. No pun intended.

"I got some extra blankets over here you can use, Yo, if you want 'em," offered Cody.

"Hell yeah. Come on with it," I responded as I got out the bed and went to the cell door.

"Aye, Yo, I gotta extra pair of thermals down here if you want them. They too lil' for me," mentioned Scurry. Low key, even though I was in a shitty situation, it was good to know that my cellies had a nigga back.

"Hell yeah, nigga, pass 'em down the wall to Cody for me, Scurry." Once they passed them down to me, I immediately slid on the thermals then tucked the blankets in front of the door cracks. "Yeah, these blankets in front the door make a big difference."

"Can you fit them thermals, Yo?" asked Scurry.

"Hell yeah, I got 'em on now. I 'preciate that Scurry, on sum."

"But shid, they should be finna have prayer call in a minute," said Scurry. "I'ma stay up for that, then after prayer call, I'm going to bed."

"You sweatin' breakfast, ain't it?" I laughed. I know the only reason that nigga was going to bed so early is so he wouldn't have any hunger pangs.

"Hell yeah, I'm hungry than a mothafucka."

"Shid, I know. I'm hungry too. I didn't even eat that

meat patty tray," I said, thinking back to that mystery substance that was on my plate earlier.

"Nigga what? You should've sent the tray down here to me, nigga. You trippin'. Listen, Yo, rule number one back here in lock-up: we don't throw no food away back here. Bones included."

I busted out laughing. "My nigga said bones and all!"

"Aite, nigga, don't think 'cuz you in that cell by yoself ah nigga can't touch ya. I'll throw some shit and piss on yo' ass on the way to the shower."

"Man, nigga, you crazy. I gotcha next time, my nigga, on sum."

"Hell yeah, Yo," chimed in Cody. "I'm wit' Scurry. We don't throw nothin' away back here, bruh."

"Aye, Cody, ion need you ridin' with me. Just wheneva Yo send that tray, you just make sure you pass it down the wall," laughed Scurry.

"Damn, Scurry! It's like dat?" asked Cody.

"Damn Scurry, my ass. Just make sure my shit make it down that wall, or it's gone be shit and piss everywhere!" Everyone in the hall started laughing. Leave it to Scurry to get everybody hyped in the most fucked up of situations.

"I tell you what, Scurry. You just throw your horse down there and get the tray from Yo like dat," Cody responded curtly.

"Oh, dat's how you playin' this shit, Cody?" asked Scurry.

"Knawl, I'm just joking, bruh."

"Y'all crazy," I laughed.

"Boy, I'm glad I'ma be at the house for Christmas this year," said Scurry as he changed the subject.

"Hell yeah. I know you is, my nigga. I don't even wanna think about that shit," I sighed.

"What you did yo' first Christmas out the joint, Yo?" asked Scurry.

"Shid nothing. I was broke as hell, so I couldn't do shit." Yeah, I still remember that Christmas vividly. I was staying at Red's house, still struggling to find a way. I remember going over to Mama place to get a plate of food, but that's about as far as it went.

"Damn, my nigga. It be like dat some time doe. So what you did yo' second Christmas out?"

"Shid me and my nigga went ova my auntie house and ate and shit. And later on dat night, I went and kicked it with a lil' female."

"So what you and the lil' chick got into dat night?" asked Scurry. His nosey ass was all in my business, but I didn't mind. Conversing with him helped keep my mind off of what was really going on.

"Man, I suppose to chill with the lil' female for a hot second then go fuck off with the gul who I was staying with at the time. But man, I ended up buying some Ciroc and got on them Watson's and shit. The next thang I know, ol' gul was waking me up asking me do I want some breakfast 'round nine in the morning."

"So what the gul you was staying with said when you came home?"

"You already know she went crazy, man. I turned my phone on that morning and had a thousand texts from her ass."

Scurry started laughing. "What the texts was saying, Yo?" he instigated.

"You already know. I ain't shit but a dog, ya hear me."

"So, what time you end up going home?"

"Later on that night. Soon as I walk through the door, she was on the bull shit. She was talkin' shit, and I told her ass you didn't know if a nigga was in a car wreck or got killed or anything. But the first thang come out yo' mouth 'bout a hoe." Ol gul was legit waiting for my ass when I walked through the door. She had on a big ass t-shirt, some pink panties, and a black bonnet. I remember I reached in for a hug and she had a real stank attitude like I just came from playing in the garbage or something.

"So, what happened after you said dat, Yo?" Scurry laughed. He sounded like he was damn near in tears at this point.

"She was like, 'Ok, you right. What happen then, Yo?' And I told her the truth. She was like, 'Bitch, I know you lyin',' and I was like, 'I told you the truth. Now leave me alone about that shit.' Then I went and got in the bed and went to sleep."

Scurry was tickled. "You crazy as hell."

"I miss dem streets doe, on everything."

"I know you do, my nigga. I can't wait to go out this bitch and have me some fun, on God."

"So dat's the gul you got locked up with?"

"Knawl, dat's another lil' female I'm talking about."

"Damn, so you just start fucking with yo' gul befo' you left the streets then? Do you still fuck with ol' gul?"

"Knawl, I stopped fucking with her 'cuz I got tired of doing her wrong. I was with her 'cuz what she could do for me and not because I love her."

"So how you broke up with her then?"

"Man, one day, Scurry, I was laying in the bed, and I just started looking at how I was living and all the people I was hurting just to make myself happy. And I just jumped up out the bed with ol' gul one night and was like, 'I can't keep living like this.' She was like, 'Living like what, Yo?' And I was like, 'The way I'm living.' And she was like, 'What you talkin' 'bout then?' I told her, 'God told me to tell you I ain't the one for you.' And I packed up my shit and left that night and never went back."

"Damn, dat crazy. What made you do dat all of a sudden?"

"Man, on God, Scurry. I ask myself dat same question. But the reason why I did it is 'cuz I knew I had her mind so gone, Scurry, and I was handling her so fuck up. She was so good to a nigga, and I couldn't keep doing her like dat 'cuz I ain't that type of nigga, ya hear me."

Scurry paused for a second. "What you was doing, Yo?"

"Shit, everything. Leaving three days at a time, got 3 or 4 niggas at the house while I'm running the streets selling dope all night, and fuckin with otha hoes... just wild shit."

"Shidddd I would've kept her ass. How many children she had, Yo?"

"None."

"Nigga you trippin'! You still got her number?" laughed Scurry.

That made me chuckle. "But on sum real shit, Scurry, I got tired of living like that. Selling dope, playing with hoe's heart, running the streets 'cuz I know dat shit was gone get me put right back in this bitch. So I was tryna start doing the right shit and get my life together so I can stay out there, ya hear me."

"I feel dat," said Scurry in a serious voice. I could tell he really meant it.

"See, Scurry, a lot of niggas... and when I say this, I'm not judging no nigga or making no excuse for myself... but a lot of niggas in the streets for fame. They don't even have to be out there; they just want that street nigga's title. But I had no choice: either the streets or starve. So I jump in that water head first, ya hear me."

"Shiddddd I know how that shit go, my nigga. Yeen gotta tell me 'cuz if I go out this bitch and shit get out of control... shit I'ma do what I gotta do to survive out that bitch."

"Prayer call! Prayer call!" somebody yelled out.

"That's prayer call, Yo. I'm finna lay back 'til they get through," stated Scurry.

"Aite, bruh. Dat's wassup."

***

"Hey, how everybody doing tonight? I'm Bruh Lacey. If anybody have any prayer requests tonight, go 'head and make them in yo' head to God in yo' cell by yo-self while I give y'all a few seconds to do so right now. Then, we will all open up with the Lord's prayer together and go on with the word The Great I Am has for us tonight. Amen?"

"Amen!" everybody responded as we all got quiet to make our prayer requests.

"Alright, let us bow our heads for the Lord's prayer," Bruh Lacey said after giving us a few seconds to say our prayer requests quietly to ourselves in our cells.

"Our Father in heaven may your name be kept holy. May your kingdom come soon. May your will be done on earth as it is in heaven, give us today the food we need and forgive us our sins as we have forgiven those who sinnd against us, and don't let us yield to temptation but rescue us from the Evil one. Amen."

"Alright, tonight I wanna talk about having faith in Jesus and having love for Jesus no matter what. Now turn yo' Bibles to 1 Corinthians 13 verse 4-7. When everybody get there, let me hear you say amen. Amen?" said Bruh Lacey.

"Amen," I responded as I found the verse.

⁴Love is patient and kind. Love is not jealous or boastful or proud ⁵or rude. It does not demand its own way. It is not irritable, and it keeps no record of being wronged. ⁶It does not rejoice about injustice but rejoices whenever the truth wins out. ⁷Love never gives up, never loses faith, is always hopeful, and endures through every circumstance.

(1 Corinthians 13:4-7, NLT)

"Now, go back and look at verse seven for a second. The first two things it's talking about is love never gives up and never loses faith. Now, all of us back here in lock-up for different reasons. Some because we got in trouble in population and had to come to lock-up. Some for protection, and some of us are facing the death penalty. But whatever reason you're back here, it's *not* the true reason you're in lock-up. Amen? See God has placed us back here tonight to hear his word. Amen? So He can get our attention 'cuz we was too busy doing us to the point God had to send us back here in these cells for 23 hours a day to get our attention. Why? Because He loves us so much, and we know that because He sent His only son Jesus Christ to die for everybody on earth befo' we was even born or did anything right or wrong. Now *that's* love.

"Think about all the things you did wrong in yo' life that God already knew you was gon' do befo' you knew what you was gone do years befo' you was born, and He still sent His only child to die for us. Now *dat's* love, and He so merciful and compassionate and for-giving, He still woke us up this morning. Amen? Be-cause He has faith in us. Now *that's* love. Let me tell y'all about me befo' I can talk about anybody else... Bruh Lacey was on the streets selling drugs. I kept a gun on me, I slept with married women, I went to pris-on for robbery and attempted murder, and God *still* loves me. Even though I got out of prison, I fell back into the same street lifestyle that got me sent to prison the first time. Then God blessed me to make it out of prison still alive, in great health, and in my right mind. And He blessed Bruh Lacey with a good wife.

"Oh, Bruh Lacey was doing his thang, but not God thang. And even doe He did all that for me... here I am again. Amen? But God love me so much, He still got me alive. Because He loves me so, He disciplines me because He's the Great I Am, King of Kings, and most of all, God is pure love. Amen? Now, turn your Bibles to Hebrews chapter 12 for me, and the title says: God's discipline proves His love. When everybody get there, can I get a amen?"

Obediently, I turned my Bible to Hebrews chapter 12 and responded, "Amen." I was ready for Bruh Lacey to continue with the word of God. I felt something stirring in my spirit as he was talking, and I wanted to get more if it.

"Now, I'ma start at verse 6 and stop at verse 13.

For the Lord disciplines those he loves, and he punishes each one he accepts as his child."[a]

[7] As you endure this divine discipline, remember that God is treating you as his own children. Who ever heard of a child who is never disciplined by its father? [8] If God doesn't discipline you as he does all of his children, it means that you are illegitimate and are not really his children at all. [9] Since we respected our earthly fathers who dis-

ciplined us, shouldn't we submit even more to the discipline of the Father of our spirits, and live forever?[b]

[10]For our earthly fathers disciplined us for a few years, doing the best they knew how. But God's discipline is always good for us, so that we might share in his holiness. [11] No discipline is enjoyable while it is happening—it's painful! But afterward there will be a peaceful harvest of right living for those who are trained in this way.

[12]So take a new grip with your tired hands and strengthen your weak knees. [13] Mark out a straight path for your feet so that those who are weak and lame will not fall but become strong.

(Hebrew 12: 6-13, NLT)

"Aite, now let's look at what God said in verse 6. For the Lord disciplines those He loves, and He punishes each one He accepts as His child. Now that go back to that word love we was talking about again. See, God loves us so much, and He is so patient and kind to us instead of giving up on us like we do Him. He punishes us and forgives us 'cuz we are His children. Amen?

"Now look at what verse 11 say. No discipline is enjoyable while it is happening–it's painful! But afterward, there will be a peaceful harvest of right living for those who are trained in this way. Now, is there anybody back here tonight in yo' lil' cell... lockdown 23 hours a day.... and most of the time 24 hours a day enjoying this? Being away from yo' family, yo' kids, and the ones who truly love us out there at home. If so, say something right now." Nobody said a word. You could hear a pen drop; it was so quiet.

"I thought so, but God loves us so much. God is still here for us even though some of us turn our back on Him and went back to the devil playground. He still here tonight talking through me to everybody back here in this lock-up tonight saying, 'I still love you, Lacey,' and everybody listening to the word of God tonight. Saying, I forgive you, just come back to me. I know you did what you did. It's ok, you still my child, and I love you. I didn't wanna punish you through this, but I had to because this the only way I could get yo' attention 'cuz the other thousand ways I tried didn't work. 'Cuz you was too busy doing yo' thang.

"You was blind to the signs and couldn't hear me or see me but guess what we do when we get in trouble? Call on God. God help me! That's the first thang we do. Then when God don't move for us like that 60-second microwave, we give up on Him. After all the times He gave us chance after chance and have the nerve to be angry at Him when He punishes us because He loves us. We not realizing how selfish we is 'cuz God won't do what we want Him to do when we want Him to. We forget about the time when we shot Jack and didn't go to jail or when we took the police on a high-speed chase, crashed, jumped out, and got away without a scratch. Not to mention all the other stuff we got away with. Instead of us recognizing the signs, we turnt up some mo'. Two months later, we done shot Mike, Blake, and Carl, so God had to sit us down to get our attention. 'Cuz this was the only thang dat was gone slow us down besides death. Amen?

"Consider giving God thanks and praise just for His love and what He has already done for us in the past already. Amen? It's time we stand up and say, 'Devil, yeah, you trick me again. But from this day forward, I'm gonna make you regret you tricking me because I'm going to be a mighty soldier for Christ like never before.' Amen? I'm not gonna let you make me mad with God no more because if I would've lived like He said in His word, I wouldn't be in this messed up situation I'm in now. But it doesn't matter because no matter what, I'ma do my best to walk with God as long as I'm alive with the attitude of a soldier for Christ. Why? Because I have the blood of Jesus flowing in my body. Amen? You see, even though we fall short and sin against Him, He is so merciful and loving. He disciplines us instead of letting us self-destruct. Now, let's look at John 10:10, if you will. When y'all get there in ya Bibles, say amen for me."

"Amen," everybody responded once we all found John 10:10 in our Bibles.

The thief's purpose is to steal and kill and destroy. My purpose is to give them a rich and satisfying life.

(John 10:10, NLT)

"Now, let's look at the thief purpose. The thief is the devil. He is the enemy, and he has a purpose in this world we live in also. Amen? Now let's see what God says His purpose is in His word. Right here in John 10:10. And His purpose is to give us a rich and satisfying life. Amen? Now, let me break it down to y'all. Bruh Lacey just got out of jail, and ain't nobody give me nothing when I come home. I ain't have no clothes or anything, but God promised me prosperity in His word. So despite how thangs look in the natural world, I gotta keep faith in His word and stand firm and be patient and believe in Him.

"So, don't worry about how thangs look in the natural because you know God loves you and always keeps His promise. He *knows* what you need. But here it is, four months later, and you still in the same position when you first got out of jail. Your blessing is coming. That's when the thief attacks your mind with lies trying to steal your faith in God's word and kill your hope and destroy your purpose with thoughts. They can be all kinds of thoughts such as, Lacey, man, you know how it go in the streets. You gotta get out and get it. You betta gone get that sack and stop playing man. You been out four months, and God ain't gave you that so-called blessing He supposed to have for you yet. Man, Lacey you crazy!

"Then, there I go. I'm back in the streets full fledge for 'bout a year or two. And the next thang I know, I'm back locked up. All the money I called myself saving I spent on making bond and getting me a lawyer. Once my judge find out I was on probation, they locked me back up with no bond. Now, the rest of the money I so-called got left, I spent it all on the store in the county jail. Two-three years later, when I get back out, I'm at square one again. Broke with nothing. But if I would've been patient and waited on God…. look what His purpose is for us. A rich and satisfying life. That's God's purpose and promise for us as His children.

"Psalm 145:13 says the Lord always keeps his promises. Amen? But I ain't gon' preach y'all head off 'cuz I know I done went 20 minutes over time. I couldn't help it 'cuz the spirit of the Lord was so strong on me. Let's end with the Lord's prayer. Everybody bow ya heads and lift ya hands with me as we end with the Lord's prayer."

We all said the Lord's prayer on one accord together in our cells, and prayer call was over with.

"What you think about that word Bruh Lacey just

preach tonight?" asked Scurry once the hall quieted down.

"The whole time he was doing his thang, I was locked in. I'm talking 'bout all ears, you hear me," I admitted.

"I told you dat nigga don't play with dat word, him or Bruh Ben."

"Bruh, I done been to church a few times with granny and my momma, and like I was telling you earlier, I went a few times on the streets and on sum, Scurry, I ain't *neva* heard the stuff I been hearing about the bible since I been locked up this time, Bruh. Straight up."

"See, Yo, like I was telling you earlier… it wasn't yo' time to see what was going on yet."

"I hear ya, Scurry, but I know I ain't dat damn blind and deaf, ya hear me." Like real shit, I don't think Scurry undestood where I was coming from. I had heard about God and church all my life, but it never really stuck with me like it is now. I don't know what it is, but something about this time is different. A *whole* lot different.

"Nigga, you crazy," said Scurry as he broke into my thoughts. "But look, turn yo' bible to Matthew 13:4 and read that."

"Aite Im fina look at it now," I said as I grabbed my

Bible and begin flipping through the thin pages. I was motivated now, and I really wanted to hear more.

"Aite, let me know when you find it," said Scurry.

"I'm there now."

"Aite, read it and tell me what you think."

This fulfills the prophecy of Isaiah that says, 'when you hear what I say, you will not understand. When you see what I do, you will not comprehend.

(Matthew 13:14, NLT)

"So what you got out of that?" asked Scurry.

"Shiddd what you was just telling me about. I couldn't see or understand 'cuz it wasn't time for me to yet."

"Damn, Yo, you might got mo' sense then I thought you did. But on some real shit, bruh, see God knew everything that was gon' happen today a thousand years ago before we was even thought about. You just gotta read yo' bible and learn 'cuz it's a lot of stuff in there that will blow yo' mind dat you don't know about. That's why you gotta study and get yo' own understanding."

"I'm already hip. Dats all I been doing since I been locked up."

"You got stories in the bible about people who went through the same thang we going through today like Moses, Joseph, King David. Shit, all them went to prison in some type of form, ya hear me. But shid, Yo, I'm finna lay it down for breakfast, my nigga. I'mma fuck witcha in the morning."

"Aite dat's wassup. I'mma fuck witcha." With that, I laid in my bed thinking about what Bruh Lacey was talking about during prayer call for a minute. It was so much to think about. I can already see that God has been trying to reach me. I was just too stubborn to notice it until now. He sent all these people, so I'm listening. After saying my prayers, I closed my eyes and let

my imagination put me to sleep.

A New Day...

"Chow call! Chow call!" the C.O. yelled as he stood in front of my cell shaking my cell door to wake me up for breakfast.

"Yeah, I'm up," I responded as I saw the tray in the C.O.'s hand. He set my food in the tray hole and walked off from my cell. Slowly, I got out the bed, grabbed my tray, and ate some runny eggs, burnt toast, and some kind of fruit cup. It wasn't much, but I was hungry from not eating anything yesterday. Once I was finished, I set the tray back in the hole and went back to sleep. I barely was sleep for what felt like 10 minutes when I was getting woke back up for lunch by another C.O. banging on my cell door.

"Yeah, aite, I'm up!" I said groggily as I woke up and noticed the C.O. standing in front of my cell again with my tray in his hand. Just like with breakfast, he sat it down then walked out. When I took off the lid, I noticed it was a meat patty. Ew.

"Oh, now. Scurry, you want this tray, bruh?" I asked.

"Hell yeah, send it down the wall!" said Scurry excitedly.

"Aite. Oh now, Cody, will you pass this tray down the wall to Scurry for me?"

"Yeah, come on with it, bruh," Cody responded. I got up off the bed and passed the tray to Cody. "Aite, I gotcha, bruh," he said as he passed it down the wall to Scurry.

"Aite, preciate it, Yo," called Scurry as he grabbed the tray.

"You good, Scurry," I responded as I sat back down on the bed and grabbed my cigarette. It was time to roll up to try to ease some of the tension I felt in my joints. My neck was hurting a little bit from how I slept the night before. I remember waking up sweating from my dream, but I couldn't recall the actual dream. Whatever it was must''ve had be spooked. *I'm finna slaughter this shit*, I thought to myself as I sat down and waited for the last chow call.

"Aite, just fuck with me when you get up," I mentioned, assuming that Scurry was about to lay it down too.

"Aite, you must finna stay up?" he asked.

"Yeah, I'm finna do me a lil' reading."

"What you finna read?"

"My Daily Bread for today and my bible."

"Oh ok. You ever read the story about Joseph in the Bible befo'?" *Was he talking about Joseph Joseph? Like Mary?* I thought to myself.

"Hell no. Where that's at in the Bible?"

"It's in Genesis. Start at Chapter 37 and read all the way to the end of Genesis."

"Aite, I'mma read it."

"Aite, dat's wassup. I'mma fuck witcha lata on when I get up for last chow."

"Cody, you gotta wick ova there burning? I need it," I asked Cody.

"Yeah, bruh, you gotta extra cigarette ova there you can spare, Yo?" questioned Cody.

"Hell no! But you can get half of this one if you want it."

"Hell yeah. 'Preciate it, Bruh."

I tore the cigarette in half and passed it to Cody as he handed me the wick. Once I finished lighting my cigarette, I passed it back then sat down on my bed to unwind and read My Daily Bread. One thing was certain. If I had down time, I was deep into this word.

"Aye,Yo," called out Dec.

"Yeah wassup," I said as I flicked my cigarette in the toilet.

"Shit, just hollin' atcha. You good, Bruh-Bruh? What you got going on over there?"

"Shit chilling."

"Oh okay. Let me know if you need me."

"Say you think you can get me one of them lil' cigarette setups for a bag of coffee on Store Day?"

"Yeah, I'll give you a setup 'til Store Day."

"Oh, you got some cigarettes ova there?"

"Yeah, I got some."

"Aite, bet. Fuck with me. I gotcha Store Day when I catch the store."

"Aite. Give me a second. I'm finna fix one up for ya real quick."

While he was doing that, I started back reading My Daily Bread. Today's lesson was more on learning who Jesus was and the different miracles that He did while he was still here on earth. I couldn't help but wonder what it would have been like to actually see God's son in action. I kind of thought about how people act today when they see someone do something great and don't even acknowledge the greatness.

"Just give me three soups off the store," said Dec. "Come to the bars one mo' time so I can tell you some real quick." Slowly, I got up off the bed and went to the bars. "Look, I gotta phone ova here too, right, and I'mma let you reach out lata on when I charge it up."

"Hell yeah. That's wassup. I need to holla at my people so I can get me some cigarettes back here. Who I gota holla at to get the cigarettes back here in lock up?" I asked with a side eye.

"The runner."

"So how much a pack of tops going for back here?"

"The same price on the land in population. $5 a pack." Well at least that part was going to be the same.

"So what the runner charge to run the play?"

"Like two or three tops; all depends on how many tops you tryna get back here in lock up. But look, I'mma holla at you lata on. I gotta handle some."

"Aite dats wassup. Fuck with me." With that, I went and sat back down on the bed and grab my Bible and started back reading about Joseph. Cody ended up letting me borrow his wick so I could light my cigarette. I started to sit back and think about the current situation I was in.

Damn this crazy as fuck. A nigga life did a whole mothafucking 360 in the blink of an eye, I thought to myself. *God please dont let a nigga life end like this,* I prayed silently as I flicked my cigarette in the toilet and continued reading the story of Joseph to keep my mind at peace and off reality until it was time to eat chow again.

***

"Chow call!" the Correctional Officer said as he walked up to my cell and set my tray in the tray hole. When I took the lid off the tray, I noticed some hot dogs, beans, a piece of cake, and a roll. *Better than that damn meat patty tray,* I said to myself as I set my tray on the bed, grabbed my cup, and went to the sink to fill it up with some water.

While I was eating, I heard Scurry trying to get my attention. "Oh now, Yo, wanna send that tray down the wall too?" he laughed.

"Hell nah," I chuckled.

"Yeah, I knew yo' ass was gon' get with the program eventually. I just hate you did it so fast. Yo' ass will fuck around and turn into dust back in this bitch while you playing," laughed Scurry.

"You crazy," I chuckled. "I'm already hip."

"You know tonight we take showers. If you want to, you can skip the shower and the police will give you a extra tray."

"I'm straight. I wanna get out this bitch for a minute anyway."

"I'mma take me a bird bath in the sink tonight." I couldn't help but bust out laughing.

"Nigga gotta survive back in this bitch forreal."

"Hell yeah. It's like we livin' on a private island back in this bitch. Shit so crazy. A nigga gotta give his shower up just so he won't be hungry. I feel like one of them homeless mothafuckaa under a bridge ova this bitch."

"Shit, when times get hard, I'mma take me one in the sink."

"Nigga yeen 'bout dat bird bath life."

"Nigga who? I done slept in abandoned houses and cars outside in the cold. I know the struggle real. But hold on real quick, Scurry, let me holla for this runner so I can ask him some befo' he leave."

"Yeen got no mirror down there in yo' cell? Cuz I don't see no runner out here, Yo. He probably gone for the night."

"How da fuck you can see if he gone or not Scurry?" I asked irritatedly. He know damn well I was stuck in this bitch just like he was.

"With my mirror. Dats why I asked you did you have a mirror down there. I gotta piece of mirror down here you can use."

A mirror? "Dats wassup. Send it down the wall for me." As I stood at the bars waiting on Cody to pass me the mirror from Scurry, the thought of how real the struggle has been for me started to go through my mind. Yeah, I still remember those times that I mentioned to Scurry. A nigga didn't have anywhere to go, so I had to walk around the block until I found a house that looked like it hadn't seen the light of day in years. I remember used to having to A-town stomp the spiders that found their way to the pallet that I made in the middle of what was probably the living room of those places. As much as that shit had me feeling low, it still didn't compare to what I was feeling up in this bitch.

"How you use this shit to see if the runner outside yo'

cell doe, Scurry?" I asked after Cody handed me the piece of mirror.

"Just stick the mirror outside yo' cell and look into it. You gon' be able to see errthang going on outside yo' cell." I reached my arm out through the bars with the mirror in my hand, and I could see up the whole hallway. I'm almost mad I didn't think about it first myself.

"This shit smooth as hell," I said as I admired my new "creation."

"Niggas in prison a mothafucka ain't it, man? They call that the third eye back here in lock-up."

"Oh ok. Dats wassup. 'Preciate it, bruh. I need this bitch."

"Yeen see the police out there on the block?"

"Yeah, I seen him taking somebody out of they cell."

"Yeah, he doing showers for tonight. Shid it probably take them 'bout 2 or 3 hours to come get you for yo' shower."

"Why you say dat?"

"Cuz we had hot dogs, so a lot of niggas gon' get in the shower. But if it was like Chicken Sunday, when we don't eat but twice a day, damn near every nigga back here gon' skip the shower." I can believe that. A real nigga be legit starving out here.

"Oh ok. Shid ian trippin'. I just wanna get out the cell for a second." Any time away from this cell was worth it at this point. They wasn't kidding when they said they never let a nigga out or anything. I think I counted the thread on my mattress like 15 times just to make time go by faster.

"I'm already hip! Shid, I done got my extra tray already and everythang. See, when the police pull up to yo' cell door with the food cart, you gotta let him know right then you wanna extra tray to buck the shower. He gon' give it to you then. You can't do it except for last chow."

"And every police back there do that shit?" I asked Scurry.

"Hell yeah."

"That's some cold-hearted shit, bruh. Knowing a nigga hungry back in this bitch, and we can't catch store but once a month. And that shit ain't nothing but $50."

"Hell yeah. They handle us fucked up. That's why we gotta stay out this jail shit."

"Yeen lyin'. The world cold, my nigga. On sum. What I'm trippin' on is I thought we was the bad guys, but these hoes fucked up, on God. I know you glad you finna get out this shit, Scurry."

"Man what? I'm sweatin' these lil' days to fly by so I can get the fuck on."

"I'm already hip. What you gon' do yo' first day out there, Scurry?"

"Shid… I'ma go chill with my momma for a hot second, then I'ma go lay up with my lil' chick for a few days."

"Hell yeah. Ain't nun wrong with that, my nigga. So who gone come pick you up?"

"My lil' chick gone come get me."

"I'm already hip. Nigga tryna smash some out the gate, ain't it, Scurry?" Shit, I don't blame him. I remember during my last lil' bid I couldn't wait to get in somebody drawers. I never was with that stuff you see in the movies about having a so-called boyfriend that was locked in there with me. Nah, I just counted down the days 'til I could be up under a female.

"Hell yeah, just to get my rocks off 'cuz a nigga been gone. But I ain't jumpin' in no relationship 'til I get myself together first. You don't remember ol' gul I used to fuck with in the county? The lil' slim chick I showed you the pictures of?"

"Scurry, you know a nigga don't remember dat shit. Dat was 20 years ago."

"Nigga, you crazy as hell! I got some pictures of her down here in the cell. I'm finna send dem ta ya."

A few minutes later, Cody was passing the photos to me of Scurry girl. "Her lil' slim ass straight," I admitted. "I'll smoke her lil' ass."

"Preciate it. Yeah she jumped out the car on a nigga in the beginning. Now I'm at the door, she wanna jump back in the car with a nigga."

"Shid, yeen gotta keep her, Scurry. I gotta car. Ask her do she wanna ride with me."

I heard Scurry start laughing. "Nigga you crazy. Send my shit back down here."

"I know dat's real. Talkin' dat shit, nigga. Yeen have to let her ass back in the car..." I laughed as I sent the pictures back down the wall.

"Aye, Yo, whateva happen with you and ol' gul who was coming to see you in the county jail? Did you fuck with her when you got out?"

"Hell yeah. I fuck with her a couple of times. That hoe crazy as hell." Mm-hmm. He was talking about Black. Black turnt out to be some straight bull shit. I would've gone to war for her at one point before she went against the code.

"Why you say dat, Yo?" asked Scurry as he broke my thoughts.

"Cuz dat hoe left me for dead in the joint. Then when I got out, she tried to act like she ain't did nun wrong. One night I was chilling with my gul, and she just up and call out the blue talking 'bout 'Wassup bae. I miss you.'"

"Oh, so yo' gul who you with now, that's who you was chillin' with when she called?"

"Naw, I was with Casey then."

"Oh, so what ol' gul said when she called?"

"Shid…. dat's why we ain't together now. When ol' gul call dat night, Casey thought we was fucking around. And it wasn't nothing I could tell her to believe we wasn't, so I was like fuck dat shit."

"Damn, so was she a rider doe?"

"Hell yeah. She rode from the time I got to Kilby until I got out."

"I know you hate that shit."

"I used to, but now naw. 'Cuz I feel like if it was meant to be, it will still be. And since it ain't, it wasn't meant to be, ya feel me?"

"Yeah, I can feel that," agreed Scurry.

"Straight up. 'Cuz if you love a nigga like you say you do, you stay down with a nigga no matter what."

"Shid, Yo. She stayed down the whole time you was in the joint, den when you got out, went left. Dirty ass nigga. Dats why dem folks got yo' ass ova there in that lil' ass cell looking crazy right there."

"Hell naw, Scurry. You some bullshit."

"But naw, on sum real shit. Shit happen like dat some time, Yo. Like you said… it wasn't meant to be."

***

"Oh now! 23 cell. You ready to go to the shower?" the C.O asked me as he pulled up to my cell.

"Yeah," I responded as I grabbed my stuff to get ready to bathe. Out the cell I went, wearing handcuffs all the way to the shower. Ten minutes later I was back in my cell.

"Yeah, wassup, Yo?" asked Scurry once I was back inside the cell doors.

"Man... that water so cold in that shower. I hurried up and got out that bitch," I complained.

"Damn, I forgot to tell you 'bout that shit," laughed Scurry.

"You laughing! A nigga a get sick as hell back here taking them cold ass showers. It's already below zero cold back in this bitch."

"I thought I told you that the water be cold as hell in the winter time and hot as hell in the summer time."

"Hell naw, nigga. You didn't tell me that. You told me how cold it get back in this bitch in the winter time and how hot it get back here in the summer time."

"Oh ok. I knew I said somethin' like that, but my bad, my nigga."

"These folks play a mean game, my nigga, ya hear me.

These folks some dirty mothafuckas. They handle a nigga fucked up, Scurry. Forreal."

Meanwhile, Dec asked me if I needed a wick to light up my cigarette. He must've read my mind because after that cold ass shower, a cigarette was just what I needed to warm myself up.

"I ain't forgot about you on the phone, Yo," said Dec after I passed him back the light. "When I get through talkin' to my wife, I'ma send it ova there so you can handle yo' business."

"Bet. Dat's wassup. Just blow at me when you ready." As I took a puff, I started thinking about who all I was finna call when I got the phone from Dec.

"Aye, Yo," called out Scurry.

"Yeah wassup?" I answered after I exhaled some more smoke.

"Nigga you still be rapping?" asked Scurry.

"Here and there but not like that."

"Yeen fuck with that shit when you got out?"

"Yeah, I went to the studio a few times while I was out there. My nigga had a studio in his house."

"Oh, yeah? I wish I knew how to rap. Nigga I'd be rich."

"That shit take money, Scurry. It's a bunch of niggas who can rap, but if yeen got the bread, that shit dead. Unless you know somebody," I added.

"Yeen lyin'. Nigga tryna get it out there, ain't it, man?"

"Hell yeah. Shit real." I leaned back and looked up at the ceiling for the thousandth time since I got here. I was starting to notice little shapes forming on the tiles. Kind of like how it is when you're looking up at the clouds for a long time and start seeing random shit. The longer I looked, the more I swear I started to see a juicy burger...

"Oh now, Yo. Come to the bars," said Dec.

"Yeah wassup, bruh?" I responded as I got off the bed and went to the bars.

"You gotta eye ova there?"

"Yeah, what you need to use it?"

"Knawl, you gon' need that to watch the block, so the police won't walk down on you while you on the phone." Damn, that's a good point.

"Oh, ok. Yeah, I got one over here."

"You ready for it now?"

"Hell yeah. Come on with it." Dec handed the phone over to Brush, then Brush slid it on over to me.

"Aite, gon' getcha 30 minutes and get outta there," said Dec as I grabbed my eye off of the table and stood at my cell door. I was on high alert, watching the block for the police as I dialed my momma's number.

"Hello?"

"Hey, Momma. What you doing?"

"Hey, boy," she said excitedly. "Momma love you. Are you ok?"

"Yeah, I'm good. I love you too, Momma."

"Momma sent you a letter in the mail, and I put $50 on yo books."

"Oh, ok thank ya momma. Where Filipe?" Filipe was my step dad. He been in the family for a good lil' minute.

"You welcome, and Filipe in there watching some game on TV."

"Oh ok. Tell him I said wassup, and I love him."

"Ok, I will. Momma been praying for you. Make sure you get on yo' knees and pray and talk to God every-day, Mario, 'cuz he the only one who can help you in yo' life right now. Do you hear me?"

"I know, Ma. I do everyday."

"And make sure you read yo' bible every chance you get, Mario. You hear me?"

"Aite, momma. I gotcha."

"So, they must didn't put you in lock-up?"

"Yeah they did, Ma. I'm in lock-up now."

"Oh you is?" she asked in shock.

"Yeah, Ma."

"Are you in a cell by yoself or with somebody else?"

"By myself."

"So, how long they gon' keep you back there in that cell by yoself, Mario?"

"Until I get done with this case, Ma," I sighed.

"And how long that's gon' take, Mario?"

"I don't know, Momma. My guess is as good as yours."

"So, how it is in there?" she asked concerned.

"Everythang is good, Momma." I knew if I told her the truth it would have her stressing. If she knew how bad it *really* was, she wouldn't be able to handle it.

"Oh ok. Well dats good."

"But I was just calling to check on you, Ma. I love you. I'll call you back when I get a chance."

"Oh ok, Momma. Love you too and make sure you call Momma back."

"Aite, Ma. Love you. Bye."

I still had a few more minutes left, so I decided to hit up my nigga Kenneth.

"Hello?" answered Kenneth as if he just woke up.

"Wassup, my nigga, dis Yo."

"Oh shit wassup, my nigga! You good?"

"I can't complain."

"You in a cell?"

"Shiddd they got me at Kilby in lock-up 'til I get through with this case."

"Damn. They got you in lock-up for that shit, bruh?"

"Hell yeah."

"So how long you gotta stay back there?"

"Shid how eva long it take me to get through with this case."

"Damn that shit crazy. Why they did that doe?"

"Cuz when you catch a capital murder on probation this what they do. Put you in lock-up until the outcome of yo' case."

"Bruh, when Lil' Mike and Scoop went back to prison for they probation violation they wasn't in no lock-up, cuzzz." Kenneth sounded skeptical, and I could tell he was probably raising his eyebrows.

"I know 'cuz they ain't have no capital murder."

"Shid... what's the difference?"

"Cuz on capital murder you can only get life without parole or the death penalty."

I heard him let out a low whistle. "Damn, bruh. I ain't know that."

"Yeah, dats how this shit go."

"Damn, my nigga. So how I go about sending you some money in there?"

"They got some shit out there called a green dot. Do you know about that shit?"

"Yeah, I know about that green dot shit. I used to send dem to Lil' Mike and Scoop ass all the time."

"Oh ok. Well that's what I need, so I can get me some cigarettes, ya here me."

"Oh, you know I gotcha, but you gon' have to wait until I get off work tomorrow at 5."

"Ok. How much you gon' send so I'll know how I need to handle my business?"

"I'ma send $50."

"Aite, that's wassup. So what's been going on out there?"

"Man, shit. The same ol' shit. Yeen missing shit out here."

"Dats wassup, my nigga. I 'preciate dat lil' money too, ya hear me."

"You good, my nigga. Just call me tomorrow 'round 8 or 8:30. I gotta go."

"Aite, love ya, my nigga," I added as I hung up the phone. *Alright, I wonder how much time I got left,* I thought to myself. I think I can make one more call...

"Hello?" said Red as she picked up on the first ring.

"Wassup, Dirty."

"Wassup, bitch," she said, thrilled to hear from me. "Why you ain't been call me, hoe?"

"I just got a chance to use the phone 'cuz I'm back in the joint now."

"Oh, they sent you to prison already?"

"Hell yeah, they violated my probation and sent me back down the road and put me in lock-up down here at Kilby."

"Damn, why they got you in lock-up doe?"

"Cuz I'm facing life without parole and the death penalty," I said, echoing my conversation with Kenneth."

"What are you serious, Yo?" she gasped.

"Hell yeah, nigga. What you think I'm playing?"

"Damn, bruh, that's crazy. You gotta get out that bitch, bruh. Forreal."

"I'm already hip."

"Damn, bruh. Shit ain't been the same since you left forreal."

"What's been going on?"

"Shit, just don't nobody come around or nun. Everybody doing they own thang."

"Oh, I thought you was talking about some mo' shit."

"Nigga you need some?"

"Hell yeah, you know what a green dot is?"

"Come on, Yo. You know I know about all that prison shit dealing with my baby daddy crazy ass."

"Yeah I forgot 'bout that shit. I should've known yo' prison ass knew what it was. Yeen nun but a ol' prison hoe anyway," I laughed.

"Oh, fuck you bitch," she grumbled.

"I'm just fuckin' witcha, Red," I responded with a smirk.

"I know it, but can I call this phone back once I get the green dot card?"

"Yeah this another nigga phone who sleep next door, but you can call back doe."

"Aite well I'm finna go get the card for you now; that's why I ask you can I call back, bitch."

"Yeah you can call back, Red, with cho' drunk big bagel lookin' ass," I laughed.

"Ion look like a big bagel hoe. Bye bitch."

Still laughing, I hung the phone up in Red's face.

Prayer Call

After giving Dec back his phone and letting him know about Red and Kenneth, I sat back down on the bed and called out to Scurry to see what he had going on.

"Yeah, wassup, Yo?" asked Scurry when I finally got his attention.

"Shit, tryna see what you got going on down there.

"Shit, down here reading my Bible."

"Oh ok, dats wassup. What you reading out the Bible?"

"Psalms. Did you ever read the story about Joseph earlier?"

"Yeah, they handled Joseph fucked up, and Joseph end up being *that* nigga. And they needed him, and he still blessed his brothers after they sold him as a slave."

"Just think how he felt when they first sold him as a slave."

"I'm already hip. They handled him fucked up. His own brothers doe…"

"That's how it be doe, but Joseph still getting glory off his story a thousand years later. That's how life is some time, Yo. We go through hard and painful times, and we don't understand at the moment. But the glory afterwards be so good and blessed it be worth it, my nigga. God don't play, my nigga. He the real whole thang."

I got quiet as I really thought about everything Scurry said, and all I knew about the story of Joseph. "Damn, dats deep Scurry."

"Prayer call! Prayer call!" Bruh Lacey yelled through lock-up letting us know he was about to begin.

"Aite, Yo. I'ma holla at you after Bruh Lacey get through doing prayer call," said Scurry.

"Aite dats wassup," I responded as I grabbed my Bible off the table and got ready for the word. I hope it was something good today...

"How is everybody doing tonight? I'm Bruh Lacey, and God gon' use me to bring us His good word tonight. Amen. If y'all will, let's take a few seconds in our cell making our prayer requests to our heavenly Father to ourselves like we do every night. Then, we will all open up in the Lord's prayer together."

After we finished in our cells and reciting the Lord's prayer, Bruh Lacey began to preach. "Alright, if y'all will, everybody turn your Bibles to Romans 11:32, and when you get there say amen."

"Amen," I murmured once I found the verse.

"Now, I was sitting down here in my cell earlier reading my word, and this verse just did some to my spirit," continued Bruh Lacey. "And I wanna share it with y'all tonight. It read,

For God has imprisoned everyone in disobedience so he could have mercy on everyone.

(Romans 11:32, NLT)

Now, God said in His word that he got us imprisoned back here in lock-up to have mercy on us, mane, 'cuz the devil was finna trick us out our soul. Amen. 'Cuz that's who we was living for on the streets—the devil, not God. But God's so merciful, and He loves us so much that He got us back here in lock-up instead of in the graveyard where we belong.

He's saying I forgive y'all, and I didn't wanna do this to y'all, but I rather y'all go through this than let the devil trick y'all out y'all soul. And y'all have to live in the lake of fire with the devil forever. Amen. And Bruh Lacey got the nerve to sit back here and complain all day to God, talkin' 'bout 'God, why my life so mess up, and why you allow this to happen to me out of all people in the world? Like, I ain't never did nun wrong in my life.' Yeah, the devil put them thoughts in Bruh Lacey head too."

He cleared his throat and continued. "Yeah, I have doubt and lost faith in Jesus some time too, 'cuz the devil at Bruh Lacey just like he at everybody back here tonight who believe that Jesus can bless them out this messed up situation we in and change our whole life around. Amen. See, now you walkin' with God and you used to walk with the devil. And he mad you walking with God now, so he trying his best to destroy us. Amen.

"So he gone try his best to steal that word of truth from you, but I'm here tonight to tell you if you believe in Jesus, no matter what things look alike around you, keep yo' faith in Jesus and live according to His word. He will bless you. So don't think just because you're facing the death penalty or life without parole God can't get you out yo' situation. The devil is a lie, and I want y'all to know tonight that nothing is too big for God to handle.

"And ain't nothing and let me say it again ain't *nothing* too big for God that He can't do for anybody back here in lock-up. The reason I know 'cuz God said in Mark 9:23.

'What do you mean if I can?' Jesus asked. Anything is possible if a person believes.

(Mark 9:23, NLT)

But Bruh Lacey, I'm facing the death penalty, and all the D.A. been offering me when I go to court is life without parole. My lawyer said he think I should take the deal 'cuz it ain't looking too good for me if I take it all the way to trial 'cuz it's a good chance I'll get found guilty and get the death penalty. But Jesus the Great I Am is the answer to all thangs. The controller, the way, the truth, *and* the light. The one who woke yo' judge up this morning. The one who woke your lawyer and your DA up this morning. He said in His word in Mark 9:23.

"What do you mean if I can?" Jesus asked. "Anything is possible if a person believes."

(Mark 9:23, NLT)

So don't tell me what nobody said 'cuz my God said He can and will do anything for me if I just believe in Him. Amen."

"Amen," I said to myself, tuned in with all ears and listening to Bruh Lacey preach the gospel.

"Do anybody hear Jesus talking to y'all tonight through the Holy Spirit living in me? He's daring us just to believe in Him tonight. Amen. He's saying yeah, you in a one-man cell 24 hours a day. Yeah, the folks treating you unfair. Yeah, you been abandoned. Yeah, you going through some pain and suffering. But whatever you believe I can do, I will do it. Amen. Now, let's turn to John 15:7, amen, and when you get there if you will, let me hear you say amen."

"Amen," I repeated once I found the verse in the New Testament.

"Now, the Word of God says:

But if you remain in me and my words remain in you, you may ask for anything you want, and it will be granted.

(John 15:7, NLT)

"Amen. Not the judge. Not the DA, but God said ask Him anything, and if you remain in Him, it would be granted. So don't tell me what the judge said or the deal the DA offered you 'cuz God said ask for certain things, and it would be granted. He said *anything*. Amen. So I don't care what nobody else said and tryna do 'cuz I already asked God and He already handled dat. I ain't worried about the DA or the judge. Amen. Dat goes back to Mark 9:23.

"What do you mean if I can?" Jesus asked. "Anything is possible if a person believes."

(Mark 9:23, NLT)

"Amen. Now you just been given the truth from God himself tonight. Amen. Now the devil's purpose is to steal this word from you tonight, and we know God got us back here in lock-up to have mercy on us 'cuz Romans 11:32 tells us so. Don't listen to dat devil and just like God talking through Bruh Lacey through the Holy Spirit living in me, the devil talking through people too through his wicked spirit living in them. He living with one of his famous prison lies and tricks saying thangs such as, 'Man I ain't finna listen to no dude in prison preach the word of God. He in prison like me, so what I'ma listen to him for.' And they don't even realize the devil using them for his work because they blind to the truth.

"The Word of God tells us that the entire world is guilty before God, and we all are sinners. That's what the Word of God says, not the prison preacher Bruh Lacey. Amen. 'Cuz I fall short every day, and I thank God for His love and mercy. In God's eyes, all sin is equal. It don't matter if you rape, kill, steal, lie, lust, or whatever sin you commit. It's all the same, and the only thang God don't forgive us for is blasphemy against the Holy Spirit. Amen."

When he said that, I thought back to all the times I heard prisoners say there's no such thing as God. I felt sorry for them. Just because I didn't go to church all the time didn't mean I ever thought he didn't exist.

"But Bruh Lacey got the nerve to talk about such and such 'cuz he did such and such like Bruh Lacey ain't no sinner or never did nothing wrong in my life," said Bruh Lacey. "And if I say I ain't, I'm calling God a lie 'cuz He said in His word not one person on earth hasn't sinned. Amen. So, Bruh Lacey can't judge nobody 'cuz I'm just as guilty as they is in God's eyes 'cuz all sin is equal to Him. Amen. So, what makes the preacher in the church different from the preacher in prison when God is using both of them to deliver His word through the Holy Spirit living in the preacher in prison and the preacher on the streets? Amen."

Hearing that made me realize that he might actually have a point. If God is going to use you, there's nothing you can do about it forreal. You can try and fight all you want, but God is going to get through to you one way or another.

"The Bible told you John the Baptist preached the word in prison, amen," continued Bruh Lacey. "Then we get to the streets; we still let that devil trick us. Talking 'bout, 'Man, I ain't going to church with all them fake folks up in there. I just seen her at the strip club last night.' Or, 'He ain't nothing but a drunk, and he be in church every Sunday. And I ain't finna give that ol' crooked preacher my money so he can buy him no new car with my money.' But God said in His word that we are all sinners—that drunk, that gul in the strip club, and that crooked preacher. The only difference between them and you is they *know* they are sinners and realize they need God. And they don't care what people like you think about them. They still gon' go to church on Sunday morning 'cuz they know they need all the God they can get in they life. They know they are sinners and they know God love them so much 'cuz he sent his only son Jesus to die for them. Amen.

"In Malachi 3:6-15... matter of fact, everybody turn your Bibles to Malachi chapter 3, and we gon' start at verse 6 and end at verse 15. When everybody get there, let me hear you say amen."

"Amen," I responded once I found <u>Malachi 3:6-15.</u> It read,

6 *"I am the Lord, and I do not change. That is why you descendants of Jacob are not already destroyed. 7 Ever since the days of your ancestors, you have scorned my decrees and failed to obey*

them. Now return to me, and I will return to you," says the Lord of Heaven's
Armies."But you ask, 'How can we return when we have never gone away?'⁸
"Should people cheat God? Yet you
have cheated me!"But you ask, 'What
do you mean? When did we ever cheat
you?' "You have cheated me of the
tithes and offerings due to me. ⁹You are
under a curse, for your whole nation
has been cheating me. ¹⁰ Bring all the
tithes into the storehouse so there will
be enough food in my Temple. If you
do," says the Lord of Heaven's Armies,
"I will open the windows of heaven
for you. I will pour out a blessing so
great you won't have enough room to
take it in! Try it! Put me to the test!
¹¹Your crops will be abundant, for I
will guard them from insects and dis-
ease.[a] Your grapes will not fall from
the vine before they are ripe," says the
Lord of Heaven's Armies. ¹²"Then all
nations will call you blessed, for your
land will be such a delight," says the
Lord of Heaven's Armies. ¹³"You have

said terrible things about me," says the Lord. "But you say, 'What do you mean? What have we said against you?' ¹⁴"You have said, 'What's the use of serving God? What have we gained by obeying his commands or by trying to show the Lord of Heaven's Armies that we are sorry for our sins? ¹⁵ From now on we will call the arrogant blessed. For those who do evil get rich, and those who dare God to punish them suffer no harm.'"

(Malachi 3:6-15, NLT)

"Now look at what God said in Malachi. Not this prison preacher Bruh Lacey, but God in Malachi. If you pay your tithes, I will open the windows of heaven for you. I will pour out a blessing so great you won't have enough room to take it in! Try it! Put me to the test! Amen.

"God said try it. Put me to the test. Amen. God said that He gotta blessing for you but because the preacher crooked, you ain't gon' pay yo' tithes. At the end of the day, God promised you He will bless you if you pay yo' tithes. But you so worried about how crooked the preacher is... you under a curse 'cuz you ain't paying yo' tithes! Look at verse 9. It says you are under a curse, amen, 'cuz you so worried about that crooked preacher to the point you missing out on yo' own blessing.

"Instead of saying I don't care what a preacher do with the money after I pay my tithes 'cuz he the one gon' have to answer to God for it, not me. Amen. 'Cuz at the end of the day, God still gon' bless me for paying my tithes 'cuz He said so in His word. So it don't matter if the preacher is stealing the money; dat don't mean God is not gon' bless me so what does it matter anyway, amen."

"Oh *now* yo come to the bars?" Dec asked me in the middle of the sermon.

"Yeah, wassup, Dec?" I asked.

"Yo' folks just texted the phone and said they got that green dot for ya. That 205-335 number."

"Aite, bet, so what I need to get from my folks off the green dot?"

"Yo' folks gon' give you 14 numbers off the back of the card. All you gotta do is write the numbers down on a piece of paper."

"Aite bet. You gon' watch the block out yo' third eye for me while I write the number down?"

"Yeah, I gotcha. Here you go," said Dec as he passed me the phone. I went ahead and called Red back, so I could get the numbers.

"What are you doing doe?" she responded.

"Nun just chilling. I was listening to the lil' prayer call they be having back here in lock-up when you texted."

"Oh ok. Well, that's good, Yo."

"I'm already hip. I 'preciate that money too, Red. On sum. You was on time with that."

"Nigga, you like my brother. You already know I'ma look out for you. You my folks."

"I'm already hip, but let me give this nigga his phone back. When I get a chance, I'ma call you so we can chop it up, ya hear me."

"Bye old Drunk Dog lookin' ass bitch."

"Man, Red, yo' ass crazy," I busted out laughing. "I love you doe, and I 'preciate that, Red, ya hear me."

When I hung up the phone, I couldn't help but smile. Red talked to me any kind of way, but she been my A1 for a good minute. She's a rare breed of friend that you just can't find anywhere.

"Oh now, Dec," I called out.

"Yeah. Wassup, bruh?" asked Dec.

"I'm through with the phone, bruh."

"Aite, come on with it." Quickly, I handed the flip-phone back to Dec.

"Aite, bruh. I got it. Did you get the numbers?"

"Yeah I got 'em."

"Okay. Do you want me to handle that with the cigarettes for you?"

Well, him doing that would help me out a lot and save me the trouble… "Yeah, that'd be straight," I said slowly

"Okay, how much is it?" asked Dec.

"It's $40."

"Oh ok. Did you write a copy of the numbers down twice?"

"Hell knawl. I'm finna do that now." I went to the table, grabbed my pen, and wrote the numbers down again on another piece of paper. Come to think of it, I should've thought of that myself.

"Hell yeah, bruh. Make sure you always write the numbers down twice just in case the runner loses the numbers or try to play games," continued Dec.

"Hell yeah. You right," I agreed. "I told my homegul to hold on to the card just in case some' happen anyway.'" I reached forward to pass Dec a copy of the green dot numbers.

"Aite, I gotcha. As soon as the runner get here in the morning for breakfast, I'ma give him the green dot numbers. And when he come back for lunch, he gon' have the cigarette for ya, bruh."

"Aite, bet."

"Aite, dats wassup. I'm finna call my wife back. I'll holla at you in a minute, Yo."

With that, I sat back on the bed and started back listening to Bruh Lacey.

"But just know God is able to help and do anything we ask of Him in His name," continued Bruh Lacey. "Back here in lock-up, all we gotta do is believe He will. Amen. And with that being said, let's close out with the Lord's prayer."

We all bowed our heads, said the Lord's prayer together, and prayer call was over with. Just like that.

"Oh now, Bruh Lacey," I called out.

"Yeah, wassup?" asked Bruh Lacey.

"Aye, man, 'preciate that word tonight. Man, that was it right there, Bruch Lacey, on sum."

"Don't thank me, man. Thank God. I ain't no different from you, bruh. That's God talking through me through the Holy Spirit, so thank Him and give Him the glory. Amen."

"Amen."

"Who this is I'm talking to anyway?" he asked.

"This Yo. Down here in 23 cell."

"Oh ok, Yo. Where you from?"

"I'm from Dolomite."

"Oh ok. I know 'bout Dolomite."

"Dats wassup. Scurry told me earlier you from Ensley, right?"

"Yeah, I'm from Ensley."

"Dats wassup, but I was just tryna let you know I 'preciate you for that word, Bruh Lacey." He just don't know how bad I needed to hear that.

"Hey, man, thank God and stay in the word, lil' bruh. And always speak blessings on everything in yo' life. No matter how the situation look, you gotta speak by faith in what you truly believe God can do. Not nobody else. Always remember that."

"What you mean by that, Bruh Lacey?"

"Aite. What they got you back here in lock-up for?"

"Cuz I caught a capital murder while I was on probation."

"Ok, so the DA tryna give you the death penalty?"

"Yeah."

"So, just like I was talking about in John 15:1 during prayer call, God said ask for anything in His name, and it will be granted, right?"

"Yeah," I responded.

"So if you ask God to send you home and you claim that by faith then He will do it by letting your words lineup with His word. By saying 'I'm going home,' or when you over there in yo' cell, just thank God for letting you go back home now. And by you doing that, you speaking things into existence by faith and you believe that God is able to do what you asked of Him. Even doe you over there in that cell with a capital murder facing the death penalty for 24 hours a day, amen, He got you."

"Amen."

"But yeah, lil' bruh, just keep the faith in God and do His will like He ask you to. In His word, amen."

"Amen. You hip me to some then, Bruh Lacey. Amen to dat."

"Amen. God taught you that. Not me, bruh, so thank Him. Stay humble and pray and talk to God all day and spend a lot of time studying His word so you can learn His laws, decrees, and regulation and His commands. Don't just read His word but *live* His word, and you a see God do some thangs in yo' life that will blow yo' mind, lil bruh."

"Aite, Bruh Lacey. I thank God for bringing me that knowledge through His Holy Spirit dats living in you tonight."

"Dats right. Anytime you need to holla at me about that Word, lil' bruh, you can. God bless."

"God bless you too, Bruh Lacey."

I was about to go back and sit on my bed, then I started to wonder what Scurry was up to. I really hadn't heard too much from my nigga.

"Oh now, Scurry," I called out.

"Yeah, wassup, Yo?" Scurry responded.

"Bruh Lacey did his thang tonight didn't it, man?"

"Yeah, I told you him and that nigga Big Ben be doing they thang with dat word."

"Yeen lying. Bruh Lacey don't play with dat word, ya hear me."

"I'm already hip."

"You finna go to sleep now, ain't it Scurry?"

"You already know a nigga finna lay it down. I'm hungry as hell too."

I couldn't help but chuckle at that. They really have a nigga back here starving. "I'm already hip," I laughed. "But I was just blowing at cha befo' you go to bed, Scurry. Holla at me in the morning when you get up."

"Aite, Yo. I gotcha. I'ma holla at cha in the morning when I get up."

"Aite."

Once I heard Scurry move away from his bars, I felt a sudden need to light up. Dec handed me the wick to light my cigarette.

"Preciate, bruh," I responded as I grabbed the wick .

"Dats wassup. You good ova there, ain't it, bruh?" Dec asked as he took the wick back from me.

"Yeah, I'm good my nigga. I 'preciate you letting me reach out and touch my people on that phone too, ya hear me. When I get straight. I'ma throw you some for the favor, ya hear me."

"Man yeen gotta give me shit for that, Yo. You good, my nigga."

"I feel that, but I gotta do that, ya hear me."

"Aite, my nigga, dats wassup. But that's already in motion. The runner gone brang dem breakfast time instead of lunch. I already called to population and gave him the numbers and every thang."

"Damn, dats wassup. 'Preciate it, my nigga."

"You good my nigga, but if you sleep when the runner brang the cigarettes, do you want me to wake you up?"

"Naw, yeen got to. I'll just get dem in the morning when we get up for lunch."

"Aite, dats wassup. I see you got folks out there that love you don't it?"

"Yeah, my nigga. I just pray God give me a chance to show them how much I appreciate them and love them too, ya hear me."

"He will, my nigga."

"This shit crazy, my nigga," I sighed. "I don't even supposed to be here, my nigga. Straight up."

"Hey, I know how you feel, my nigga."

"I'm talking 'bout I was just at the house with the kids and my gul... kickin' it. And in the blink of an eye, these mothafuckas got me living in a basement 24 hours a day, ya hear me."

"Hey, I know how you feel, my nigga. I talk to my wife and kids every day, and dat don't do nun but make it worse."

"I can't wait to talk to my gul, ya hear me."

"Why you ain't call her tonight when I let you use the phone?"

"Cuz she locked up right now too."

"Damn. Y'all must be on the same case together?"

"Naw, she lock-up for some mo' shit."

"Oh ok. So how many kids you and yo' gul got?"

"Nun. I don't have no kids. My gul got four doe."

"Oh ok. Shit I know you love her. Shit.... four kids," laughed Dec.

"Hell yeah I love dat crazy motherfucka to death, ya hear me."

"Shid I'm already hip. You fucking with her and she got four kids. And you ain't got nun. Shit, dat ain't nun but love."

"Hell yeah. I miss they ass too."

"Hey, I miss mine too, my nigga."

"So who go the kids while yo' gul in jail?"

"Her mama."

"Oh ok. Well that's good."

"I'm already hip. But say, Dec, how much dem phones be going for?"

"A touch screen $350 and a flip phone $200. You must tryna get you a phone?"

"Yeah, I want to."

"Shit, you can use this phone," Dec offered.

"I'm already hip, but ain't nun like ya own shit, ya hear me."

"True, but shit. You finna be going back and forth to

court, and if you leave it with a nigga when you go to court, he might be gone when you get back or get jam up with that motherfucka. So dat's a loss all the way 'round."

"Yeen lyin'." I guess he did have a point.

"Hell yeah, my nigga, you gotta think about that shit. I'm already hip, just chill and see what the folks gon' do nigga. Yeen even got yo' indictment papers yet is it?"

"Hell naw, not yet."

"That's what you gotta wait on 'cuz I done seen niggas go home from back here like that on they case because the grand jury throwed they case out for lack of evidence."

"Damn forreal?" I didn't know that was a thing. That gave me a little more hope.

"Hell yeah."

"So how long it take yo' indictment papers to come back from the grand jury while you back here."

"Shit, it can take anywhere from 6 months to a year."

"Oh ok."

A few minutes later, I heard footsteps approaching my cell. Instinctively, I backed up and sat on my bed. As soon as I kicked up my feet, I saw a red-headed white man standing at my door. He was a short guy and looked like he didn't get out much.

"What's yo' name and A.I.S. number?" the Correctional Officer asked me as he walked up to my cell door.

"Demario Jones. 267787."

"Here you go," he responded as he handed me my mail. As he walked away, I looked down at the envelope and noticed it was a letter from my momma.

"Yo, he just gave you some mail?" asked Dec.

"Hell yeah, my momma sent me a letter."

"What Mama talking 'bout?"

"God. You know how a nigga Mama be."

"Hell yeah, my nigga. I wish my momma was still living, my nigga."

"Damn. Hate to hear dat my nigga, ya hear me."

"I don't even know what made me say dat, but it's all good, my nigga, 'cuz it was her time, bruh."

"True. That's why I gotta do some with my life, so I can look out for my momma befo' it's too late. All the shit I done put her through… I feel like I owe her dat."

"Hell yeah. I know how you feel, my nigga, straight up."

"Hell yeah and out of all my momma kids. I'm the only one who stay in some shit, ya hear me."

"Oh yeah? How many kids yo' momma got?"

"It's four of us." Yeah, my other siblings were cool, but we weren't as close as I would like us to be. It just feel like we come from separate worlds.

"Oh ok. I got one brother and one sista. But look I gotta handle some. I'll holla at you tomorrow. You need anything else befo' I kick back?"

"Yeah, let me get a light befo' you fall back." I grabbed a cigarette, got off the bed, and went to the bars to get the wick from Dec. Few minutes later, I was back down on the bed smoking my cigarette. I found myself deep in thought about what Dec said about niggas going home from lock-up because the grand jury threw their case out due to lack of evidence. "Damn that will be a miracle," I said to myself as I sat on my bed and drifted into a sleep.

6 months later:

"Name and A.I.S. number?" the Correctional Officer asked me as he walked up to my cell door. It was the same one who gave me the letter from Mama a few months back.

"Demario Jones. 267787," I responded as I got up off the bed to see what the C.O. wanted.

"You got legal mail. Sign right here."

I grabbed the pen from the C.O. and signed my name.

"Alright, that's it," he responded as he handed me my envelope and walked off.

I wonder what this is, I thought to myself as I sat back down on the bed and opened my mail. As I skimmed through the paper, I saw that it was my indictment papers from the grand jury. I had been indicted on four counts:

Count 1: murder/robbery

Count 2: murder/kidnapping

Count 3: murder/in vehicle

Count 4: murder/out vehicle

"What the fuck?! "This shit gotta be wrong," I said to myself. I was completely lost for words and confused.

"Oh now, Dec," I called out as I got off the bed and went to the bars.

"Yeah, wassup, Yo ?"

"Come to the bars. Man, look at this shit." I passed Dec the indictment papers to make sure my eyes weren't playing tricks on me.

"Damn, my nigga. You wasn't bull shittin' out there was it?" said Dec as he read the papers.

"Nigga, that shit wrong. Bruh, I caught one cap case. Bruh, I don't know where the other three cases pop up from."

"Oh, so when you first got locked up on yo' 'case, you only had one capital murder?"

"Hell yeah."

"Oh well somebody had to tell them folks some in order for them to indict you on three mo' counts, bruh. Straight up."

"Why you say dat?"

"Cuz they came back and indicted you on three more counts, so they got somebody saying something. That's how them three more counts pop up."

"These folks tryna hang a nigga forreal."

"Hell yeah. Here you go doe," said Dec as he passed me my indictment papers back. "Yo, do you gotta paid lawyer on yo' case?"

"Hell naw. I got two court appointed lawyers."

"Damn, bruh. You might need to figure out a way to get you a paid lawyer somehow 'cuz dem court appointed lawyers will sell yo' ass out, bruh."

"Man, Dec, I ain't sweatin' them folks. I'm blessed, my nigga. God got me, my nigga, ya hear me." At this point, I was speaking by faith. I knew good and well that the problem was out of my control. With four counts of capital murder, I had two choices. Either I trust God and believe in Him, or give up and let the devil win.

"Damn, nigga. You got some strong faith, my nigga, forreal. Damn."

"I'm blessed, Dec, ya hear me. I ain't finna worry about that 'cuz that ain't nothing but the devil tryna steal my joy, ya hear me."

"I ain't gone lie; you a strong-minded young nigga, my nigga. Forreal. Man, them folks just indicted you on four counts of capital murders, and you acting like you just got four D.U.Is or something."

"Nigga, you crazy," I laughed.

"But naw, on some real shit, if that was me in yo' shoes, I'll be over there in that lil' ass cell going crazy. I'm damn near twice yo' age."

Damn, I didn't realize Dec was that old. "Shit, Dec, I either can be over here going crazy or leave it in God hands, ya hear me. I'm just gone leave it in God's hands, and the enemy don't like dat. Dat's why the devil attacking me 'cuz I'm standing strong on my faith in God. The devil tryna steal my peace and my faith, but I prayed and ask God to bless me out my situation using His name and God said in John 14:14:

Yes, ask me for anything in my name, and I will do it!

(John 14:14, NLT)

And I believe He will do what I have ask of Him in His name. I refuse to believe anything else, and God has already won the victory for me. I claim dat in Jesus's name. Amen. And I thank Him for it already, ya hear me."

"Dang, nigga, I see you been over there in that Bible. Damn, you got super faith."

"You gotta speak it into existence and believe you receive what you ask for, and you will, ya hear me."

"Ok, I hear ya ova there, young nigga. Ain't nun wrong with that. You been over there reading that Bible forreal, my nigga. I can tell."

"That's all I be over here in my cell doing, my nigga. Ever since Scurry left and went home, then you be over there on the phone all the time doing yo' thang, so I just be over here praying and reading my Bible all day 'til Bruh Lacey have prayer call. Then after that, I get in the bed and go to sleep, ya hear me."

"I notice that too. When Scurry left and went home. I thought you was over there losing yo' mind in that cell for a minute 'cuz you was so quiet ova there. That's why sometime I'll holla ova there and ask you is you straight over there."

I'm already hip, Dec, ya hear me. Man, I know this might sound crazy, but on some real shit, dis the most peaceful I felt in my life since I been over here in this cell, bruh."

"I can tell too, my nigga. You don't even ask to use the phone or nothing no mo' forreal."

"That Bible, my nigga."

"Dis my gul calling, Yo. I'ma get back witcha in a minute."

"Aite. Go 'head and handle ya business. I'm finna lay it down for tonight anyway, ya hear me."

"Aite, bruh. Keep ya head up, my nigga."

"Aite, you too. my nigga. God bless ya."

***

"So what you got going on ova there, bruh?" Cody asked as he handed me the wick to light my cigarette. It was the middle of the day, and I just finished eating lunch.

"Im just coolin' at the moment. I'm finna do me a lil' reading in a minute. Wassup," I responded as I continued smoking my cigarette on the bed.

"I was just hollin' at cha, bruh, to be forreal. I heard you talking to Dec last night about your indictment papers. Dat shit fucked up, bruh."

"Oh, errthang good, Cody. I'm blessed, ya hear me." I flicked my cigarette in the toilet.

"I'm already hip, Yo. Just know if you ever need to talk to me, dude, feel free any time."

Why this nigga actin' like I'm on death row or some shit? "Dats wassup," I laughed. "Why you all sad and shit, Cody? I'ma be aite. God got me. I'm blessed, ya hear me."

"I know, bruh, 'cuz you a good dude, 'bruh."

"Ain't nobody good but God, Cody, ya hear me."

"Yeah, bruh. I hear ya."

"But check this out, Cody. I'm finna fall back for a second, ya hear me."

"Aite, bruh. Holla at me later."

"Aite," I responded as I grabbed my Daily Bread and my Bible and began studying until I fell asleep.

"Oh now, Yo. Wassup, bruh? Dec asked me as I sat on the bed eating my food.

"Nun, just woke up. Ova here eatin'," I said as I stuffed a forkful of undercooked vegetables in my mouth.

"Yo, it shouldn't be too much befo' the folks come get you for court now."

"How you know dat?"

"Cuz they just sent you them indictment papers and usually after dat, they come get you for court."

"Oh ok. Shid dats wassup. I'm ready to get out this cell for a minute anyway.".

"Hell yeah, my nigga. I know you is."

Man, he had no idea...

Two months later:

"Demario Jones?" the Correctional Officer called as he walked up to my cell door as I was reading my Bible.

"Yeah, wassup?"

"You on transfer for court in the morning. Put all yo' stuff inside these two brown bags and put them inside your laundry bag so in the morning, the Officer will put them in the property room for ya." He set the two brown bags in the tray hole.

"Aite, dats wassup," I responded as I got up off the bed and started packing my stuff up.

"Oh now, Yo," called out Dec.

"Yeah wassup?" I asked as I picked up my toothbrush.

"You headed back to court, ain't it?"

"Hell yeah. I'm ready to get me a lil' air too, ya hear me." I couldn't remember the last time I was able to let the sun really hit my face.

"I'm already hip, my nigga," laughed Dec in agreeance. "Good luck, bruh."

"Preciate it, my nigga."

"Shit, you'll be gone first thang in the morning. When Jefferson County drop they chain off, they gon' pick you up and take you back with them. Now, I gotta hope they put somebody ova there in that cell who laid back like you."

"Ain't nun but one of me, my nigga, ya hear me. But naw errthang gone be good just think positive, ya hear me."

"Here you go, Yo, with this Martin Luther King shit," laughed Dec.

"Man, nigga you crazy." Even though I ain't really know bruh like that, I was gon' miss him. He definitely looked out for me since I been in this cell.

"Damn, Yo. Man I'm glad to see you go, but I'm mad to see you go at the same time," confessed Dec.

"Shiddd they probably put me back in this same cell doe," I reassured him.

"That's one out of a hundred. You probably end up on the other side of lock-up or some shit."

"Probably will," I admitted. "I ain't trippin', ya hear me."

I started folding up the couple of clothes I did have in there with me. Socks, underwear, pants...

"Oh now, Yo," called out Cody.

"Yeah wassup?"

"You gone in the morning ain't it?"

"Hell yeah."

"Dat's wassup. Keep ya head up, bruh."

"Dat's wassup. You too, bruh, ya hear me. I'ma be praying for y'all, ya hear me."

"Dats wassup, bruh. I'ma be praying for you too, bruh."

"Oh now, Yo," called out Dec in the middle of me and Cody's conversation. "Do you wanna call yo' folks and let them know you finna go back to court?"

"Naw, I'm good," I said as I put the last item in the bag. "My momma sleep right now 'cuz she gotta get up and go to work in the morning. I'ma call her tomorrow when I get to the county jail."

"Oh ok dats wassup."

"I know you ready to go back to the county so you can see yo' folks on that visitation yard, ain't it man?"

"Hell yeah. I'm sweatin' to see my gul ass. I hope she out, ya hear me."

"I'm already hip," said Dec as he took a pull from a cigarette. "You got all yo' shit packed up ova there yet?"

"Hell yeah. I pack dat shit up ASAP ya hear me."

"A nigga be glad to get out these cells for a second don't it, man," laughed Dec.

"Hell yeah," I responded.

"Well, it won't be long now, Yo. You gone in the morning."

"I'm already hip. I'ma stay up and listen to Bruh Lacey do prayer call, then I'ma lay it down for the night."

"Shiddd Bruh Lacey should be finna do prayer call now. By the time you get back from court, it should be a lil' warmer outside. Hopefully these folks will start taking us outside for our walk. That way we will have a chance to chop it up when you get back if you ain't on this side of lock-up."

"Hell yeah. Hopefully they will."

"Prayer call! Prayer call!" Bruh Lacey's voice echoed through lock-up, letting us know he was about to begin.

"Aite, Dec. I'ma blow back at cha after Bruh Lacey get through doing prayer call, ya hear me."

"Aite, Yo, dats wassup."

With that, I grabbed my Bible off the table, sat down on the bed, and got ready to hear the final word I would get before I was transported.

"How is everybody doing tonight? I'm Bruh Lacey, and God got a message for us tonight. But if y'all will, at this time, let's take a few seconds in our cells to make our personal prayer request to our heavenly father to ourselves like we do every night. Amen. Then we will all open up with the Lord's prayer together. Amen."

As the block got quiet, I started thinking about all the people I had on the outside. *Lord, if it's in your will, please let me have the chance to be with them again,* I prayed silently.

"Alright, if you will, turn ya Bibles to Isaiah 61:1 for me, and when you get there, let me hear you say amen," said Bruh Lacey.

"Amen," I said in a low voice as soon as I found the verse.

"Alright, listen to what the Lord said in Isaiah 61:1," started Bruh Lacey as he read the scripture out loud.

The Spirit of the Sovereign Lord is upon me, For the Lord has anointed me to bring good news to the poor. He has sent me to comfort the brokenhearted and to proclaim that captives will be released and prisoners will be freed.

(Isaiah 61:1, NLT)

"Now *God* said that. Not Bruh Lacey, but *God* said he come to bring good news to the poor. Amen. So when He said that right there, I knew he was talking to Bruch Lacey then," laughed Bruh Lacey.

"Amen, then He go on to say He come to comfort the broken hearted and to proclaim captives will be released and prisoners will be freed. Amen. I know you sayin', 'Bruh Lacey I know God said that in Isaiah 61:1, but the judge just gave me death row.' And, 'Bruh Lacey, I got life without parole.' But God said in Mark 9:23,

"What do you mean, 'If I can'?" Jesus asked. "Anything is possible if a person believes."

(Mark 9:23,NLT)

"Amen, and God just told you the prisoners will be freed. Now all you gotta do is believe. Amen. He didn't say certain kinds of people in prison; he said prisoners. Amen. People come off death row and life without parole all the time and go home, so don't tell me what God can't do. Amen. The creator of all thangs. My father. My rock. My answer to all my problems. Amen. So quit worrying about what the D.A. said and the judge and ya homboys said. 'Cuz if God don't wake them up in the morning, then what you see our Father is the controller of all thangs on earth and don't nothing happen without the head honcho say so. Amen.

"Ain't no limit to what God can do. He can do any and all thangs, amen. If you will, turn to Isaiah 43:34. When you get there, let me hear you say amen."

"Amen," I said as I flipped to the verse.

"Alright, and the Lord said in Isaiah 43:3-4

³For I am the Lord, your God, the Holy One of Israel, your Savior. I gave Egypt as a ransom for your freedom; I gave Ethiopia[a] and Seba in your place. ⁴ Others were given in exchange for you. I traded their lives for yours because you are precious to me. You are honored, and I love you.

(Isaiah 43:3-4, NLT)

"Amen. God said He traded lives for His people because they was precious to Him, amen. You see, when Moses and the Israelites was in trouble with their enemies, the Egyptians and Pharaoh didn't wanna let God's people go. God departed the Red Sea for His people to escape from their enemy, and when the Egyptians and Pharaoh chased behind God's people through the Red Sea, He closed the Red Sea back up on Pharaoh and the Egyptians.

"Once His people made it on dry ground and drowned all the Egyptians and Pharaoh in the Red Sea, Hebrews 13:8 says,

Jesus Christ is the same yesterday, today, and forever.

(Hebrews 13:8, NLT)

"Amen. So you see that same God He was and did for His people back then? That's the same God today for us, and He will do dem same thangs for us today in our life 'cuz He said so in His word. And Psalm 145:13 says,

For your kingdom is an everlasting kingdom. You rule throughout all generations. The Lord always keeps his promises; he is gracious in all he does.

(Psalm 145:13, NLT)

"The Lord always keeps His promises, amen. And God don't lie, so every word in His word is a promise. Amen. And God will do the same miracles for us today and Mark 9:23 says,

'Anything is possible if a person believes,' amen. But if you will turn your Bibles to 1 Peter 4:12-13 for me, and we'll be through for tonight. Amen."

Bruh Lacey cleared his throat and continued with the word. "Alright, and the title reads 'Suffering for being a Christian.' Amen. See God just told you in His word you was gon' suffer for being a Christian. But why when we go through a lil' suffering, we turn our nose up at God? Amen. Now let's look at what God said in His word.

¹² Dear friends, don't be surprised at the fiery trials you are going through, as if something strange were happening to you. ¹³ Instead, be very glad—for these trials make you partners with Christ in his suffering, so that you will have the wonderful joy of seeing his glory when it is revealed to all the world.

(1 Peter 4:12-13, NLT)

"Amen. God said don't be surprised of the thangs you are going through. He said, instead, be very glad 'cuz God knows through your suffering, it strengthens you and makes you stronger and rooted in Him, amen. But

I wanna encourage everybody to be patient and keep up faith through the suffering and realize suffering means you are God's child. When you walking with Him, just hold on and keep the faith in Him. No matter how thangs look and get rough, stand firm and tough in the Great I Am's word. Amen. But remember, spend time with God every day and feed your spirit daily with the word of God so when that devil attack you, you'll be full of the word of God. Amen. But with that being said, let us bow our heads for the Lord's prayer and close out for tonight, amen."

We all said the Lord's prayer together and prayer call was over with.

"Oh now, Dec," I called out.

"Yeah, bruh. Wassup, Yo?" said Dec in a raspy voice like he was just dosed off.

"Nun, just blowin' at cha befo' I lay it down."

"Oh ok. Ion got shit going on ova here. I just got off the phone with my wife. Shid, I'm finna get ready to lay it down too," Dec responded.

"Oh ok dats wassup. I was just hollin' atcha cuz I know y'all niggas gon' be sleep when I leave for court in the morning, ya hear me."

"Dats wassup, my nigga. Keep dat same positive mind-set, bruh, and stay in that Bible, bruh."

"Oh you already know dat, ya hear me."

"Dats wassup, bruh. I 'preciate you hollin' at me befo' you go, but I'm finna lay on back for the night."

"Dats wassup, my nigga. God bless ya, bruh, ya hear me."

"God bless you too."

"Oh now, Cody," I called out, but I didn't get a response. *He must be sleep,* I thought to myself. So, I laid in the bed, said my prayers, and went to sleep. The next day would start a new chapter in this journey that God was taking me on. I didn't know what to expect. All I knew was that I had to trust Him, and let whatever happen....happen.

Stay tuned for the next book of
this three part series titled:

The Testimony of the
Dead Man Walking

Part 2: Judgment

Made in the USA
Columbia, SC
13 January 2022

53580250R00124